This paperback edition published in 2021 by

Little Toller Books
Ford, Pineapple Lane, Dorset

First published in 1948 by Max Parrish & Co

ISBN 978-1-908213-75-4

Text © The Estate of Geoffrey Grigson 2021
Photographs © The Estate of Percy Hennell 1948

Jacket © The Estate of John Piper 1985

Introduction © Ed Kluz 2021

Typeset in Sabon by Little Toller Books
Printed in UK by TJ Books

All papers used by Little Toller Books
are natural, recyclable products made from
wood grown in sustainable, well-managed forests

A CIP catalogue record for this book is available
from the British Library

1 3 5 7 9 8 6 4 2

AN ENGLISH FARMHOUSE

AND ITS NEIGHBOURHOOD

Geoffrey Grigson

Photographs by Percy Hennell

LITTLE TOLLER BOOKS

Chalk, with brick, on the east wall of a farmhouse,
in good condition after more than 250 years.

CONTENTS

High Applegarth Farm, Swaledale, North Yorkshire, shortly before building work began in 1986. Ed Kluz's mother and brother walk below the remaining portion of the building showing outlines of rooms and cupboards belonging to the demolished wing which came down sometime around 1900.

INTRODUCTION

Ed Kluz

→⟩⟩⟨∷ ═══════ ⟩⟨⟨⟨←

T HERE IS, to me, something immediately recognisable about the
landscape of ancient tracks, field patterns and buildings over which
the poet Geoffrey Grigson casts his eye in this intimate portrait of place
and decay. Although the true identity of 'Ashton' is elusive, perhaps to
broaden the relevance or liberate it from being associated with the book,
the village and the landscape he describes very much existed. And much
like the fictional Ashton, the origins of my own childhood home – a
remote hamlet, called Applegarth, sited a few miles west of the Yorkshire
market town of Richmond – also stretch back a thousand years, possibly
further, to a point beyond the time of the Romano-British farmers who
built their fortified dwelling below the overhanging sand and limestone
cliffs. So much of what Grigson describes resonates with my own
memories of the hillside where I grew up, a borderland that I return to
and wander in my mind's eye.

> Up above, a flat plateau, a wintry landscape without much timber, down
> below, a more genial, summery landscape, gently rising and falling, much
> planted with elms, and much of it old grassland upon clay – grassland little
> disturbed by the ploughing campaigns of the Second World War.

When my parents bought the perilously ruined remains of a farmhouse at Applegarth in 1986, strange disjointed vestiges of its previous life persisted. Flakes of red oxblood distemper hinted at the cold comforts and simple luxuries of rooms that had long since rotted and collapsed into a morass of fallen timbers, dead sheep, animal faeces, nettles and barbed wire. The vestiges of past human presence revealed themselves in the discovery of surprising objects: a bright-white, near pristine ceramic decoy egg, intended to encourage hens to lay, lifted from the desiccated filth of a collapsing wall; a neat stack of blue and white china bowls, carefully placed in the earth by hand and shattered by the bucket of a blundering mechanical digger; an empty whisky bottle found hidden behind a beam in the roof bearing the label of a local inn destroyed by fire in 1908. Still-life cameos speaking of lives spent.

To understand the derelictions at Applegarth, or the many thousands of ruined farm buildings like those in Ashton, one has to untangle agricultural history in Britain and follow the complex threads through centuries of fluctuating fortune, which so often come to an end after the Second World War. The decline of rural communities began with Enclosure, followed by the rapid industrialisation and urbanisation of the nineteenth century. The lure of employment in these growing county towns and cities gradually leached the labour force from the land, depriving farms of work-horses. Added to this were the long-term destabilising effects of the Corn Laws repeal in 1846, which up until this point had served to protect the interests of domestic grain production, but now left the UK market vulnerable to cheaper imports and the inherent risks of international trade.

Over the following hundred years several subsequent acts of parliament sought to embrace the opportunities of a peacetime global market, and when necessary protect the interests of food production and security on home turf during periods of conflict. Initiatives towards the end of both the First and Second World War helped to underpin farming activity, resulting in mini agricultural booms. However, by the late 1940s, the multifaceted ecosystems of small-scale and mixed farms, which had once populated rural Britain and shaped such hamlet communities as Ashton and Applegarth, had almost entirely vanished, along with the biodiversity in these landscapes.

Applegarth bore testament to this slow hundred-year decline: collapsed field boundaries, derelict structures and neglected smallholdings dotted the hillside. Our farmhouse, built sometime around 1800, was the last portion of what had once been a much larger building. The remaining barn, being the most useful and practical part, was retained whilst the majority of the abutting domestic wings had been pulled down at the turn of the century. The scars of rooms – fireplaces, cupboards, floors – could still be plotted out in the remaining plaster which clung to the exterior walls of the barn. As observed by Grigson, buildings in their decay often reveal a palimpsest of layers in which previous purposes and the truer nature of their structure can be decoded and unravelled. His almost forensic autopsy of the various buildings at Ashton reveals the deep-rootedness of their vernacular – the line between landscape and architecture becomes blurred, and a view of the farmhouse as a living organism emerges, one that is symbiotic with its surroundings. The farm is both a child and parent of the land.

In exploring Ashton, Grigson's steady guiding focus on the particularities of vernacular materials and architecture betrays a life-long passion for archaeology and geology, while his descriptions blend cool modernity (lichenology, concrete, galvanised metal) with prose more akin to the visionary pastoral traditions of William Blake and Samuel Palmer. The keen rendering of his observations and overlaying of history, purpose, pattern and form is no sentimental journey into some imagined past, but an inquiring exploration of the realities of what he knows to be, or have been. It is the rediscovery of an old country seen through the near-opaque and profound trauma of the Second World War.

The significance of Grigson's exploration into the deep recesses and minutiae of a corner of England is clear when understood in the context of the postwar era. *An English Farmhouse*, first published in 1948, demonstrates the vital part he played in splicing together the sentiments of an earlier Romanticism with the fresh clarity of European Modernism; which fed into the British Neo-Romantic movement of the early twentieth century. His collaboration with like-minded artists and poets such as John Piper, John Craxton, W. H. Auden and Dylan Thomas, led to the publication of the influential *New Verse* anthologies and seminal *The Poet's Eye*. As a result of his sometimes volatile critical and creative interactions with friends and contemporaries, his sensibilities were honed into a multifaceted lens through which he reflected the world around him.

Previous to the book's publication, both of his collaborators on this project had been engaged in documenting the scars of conflict: John Piper as an official war artist recording the shattered sites of bomb damage and Percy Hennell as a photographer capturing images of reconstructive facial plastic surgery. The split-second destruction which they had all witnessed differs from the slow, even comforting, decay captured in this book. I wonder whether the act of pulling form and meaning from the abstract and rich matrix of decay observed at Ashton is in some way a process of healing, regathering in the face of so much uncertainty?

There is a meditative rhythm found in among the ruins of *An English Farmhouse*, in the observations and words of Grigson which rock the reader into the fluxes of the past and stillness of stone, earth and land. Its complex narratives also chime with the current concerns of ecology, sustainability, farming practices and the changing nature of rural communities. There are old voices to be listened to here, in the structures, materials, surfaces, texture and scatter of residual objects of life and occupation. Like Grigson's writing, they form a complex and abstract matrix which vibrates and resonates somewhere between the intangible unknowns of the past, the hard reality of the present and the fragile inevitability of the future.

Ed Kluz
Bath, 2021

PREFACE

Geoffrey Grigson

Tᴀɪs ʙᴏᴏᴋ is mainly about the stony and wooden details of a farmstead, in the south of England, which I have called Ashton Farm; near a village which I have called Netton. It would not be quite true if I were to say that Netton and Ashton Farm do not exist; but it is true that they are not to be found on the Ordnance Map. The Ashton Farms are changing rather faster than the people who live in them. Many of the farm buildings I have written about and several that we photographed have collapsed since this book was begun. With each one of them a piece of social history collapsed as well. The buildings that replace them – if buildings do replace them – are not natives, of native conception and native material. They belong, as the people belong without quite realising it, to a new nativity, to a much larger, looser and, so far as it has developed, a less seemly context.

To our eyes, the old local context of farm and farmhouse and farmworker's cottage is familiar enough – from the far view; but to discover how such buildings were made, out of what tradition they emerged, one must bring one's eyes to the unfamiliar view, close up to stone, thatch, oak, weatherboard, even galvanised iron; until one sees the grain and the shape, as well as the total.

These surface details (which added up make that familiar far view) have their own peculiarities of attraction, their own validity. Many of them illustrated or described in this book would not have been seen without the exploratory, dictatorial vision of my friends John Piper and Percy Hennell, who have shivered patiently outside ruins waiting for clouds to release the revealing vividness of light.

The conception of such a book, illustrated in such a way, was John Piper's; but he is not to blame, nor is Percy Hennell, for any notions of my own (not all of which will be acceptable notions) about the present and the future of farming in such a district as I have described; nor is either of them to blame for any of my errors.

We believe that colour photography can be revealing without being chromatically hideous. Blue skies, generally, have been cut away. That skies have such a colour we do not need to be told, *ad nauseam*, by plate after plate. We include no wide view of the farm – there have been colour plates enough of typical farmsteads; but bringing the camera close up to a quoin, to a piece of paving, to an elm fence, to a patch of lichen – that may reveal what the normal use of cameras does not incline one, certainly does not train one, to notice.

I have lifted information and illumination about building technique and tradition from several books and from various memoirs of the Geological Survey; from S. O. Addy's *Evolution of The English House*, and C. F. Innocent's *Development of English Building Construction*; from J. A. Howe's *Geology of Building Stones*, his and J. V. Elsden's *The Stones of London*, from John Watson's *Cements and Artificial Stone*, and from *The Village Carpenter*, by Walter Rose.

Mr H. C. Brentnall, FSA, kindly lent me his pamphlet, published in 1930, on sarsen stones. I have used volumes of the English Placename Survey; and I am grateful to the work of several writers on the countryside, especially Mr C. S. Orwin, J. W. Robertson Scott (*The Dying Peasant*) and the late George Sturt; grateful also to many friends in the district of 'Ashton Farm', who will raise their eyebrows rather high at some of the views I have adopted or developed.

Geoffrey Grigson
Ashton Farm, 1948

An
ENGLISH
FARMHOUSE

Geoffrey Grigson

A lump of sarsen abandoned by the track between the downs and the farm.

THE NEIGHBOURHOOD

LORD ERNLE began his celebrated book on the history of English farming from a double conviction: that land nationalisation would be bad for England, and that more peasant ownerships would be 'economically and agriculturally' advantageous. My own conviction is neither here nor there, since I am neither an agriculturist nor an economist. The farmhouse and farm buildings that this book deals with, and the other farms all around, have grown out of the historical process that Lord Ernle describes. They still exist, though most of them are in decay. They are out of date, they are little suited in many ways to the needs of the farmers who use them, or to the possibilities of a scientific agriculture. They are Antiques, like the village church; and I do not make any claim, political or economic, for their perpetuation or the perpetuation of the system they have been produced by. But they are objects with a history of legitimate fascination. They are pleasing (partly because of their decay) to look at. They still exist and, belatedly and half-heartedly patched, they will exist for some few more years, in spite of dry rot and bad thatching and discontent and old-fashioned farming.

First of all, I shall describe, rather than name, the district, the stretch of countryside into which the farmhouse has grown. The district has its distinctions and peculiarities, scenically and geologically. But my aim is to present what is roughly general and English by what is detailed and peculiar, if only to illustrate the general fact that districts in England are the same, that each district's peculiarity is part of its Englishness. This

stretch of country is in the South – south of London, which lies some
seventy miles away. It is cut by no great main road, and lies some miles from
a main line. It is not scenically either dull or tedious; it is not celebrated
for its beauty. The farmers and the village people live their own lives, have
few visitors, except from RAF camps, and let no rooms. This is not a self-
conscious part of the country.

The key to the scene is a long, low escarpment, sometimes a cliff,
which runs roughly north-east to south-west. The escarpment is the
border between two landscapes. Up above, a flat plateau, a wintry
landscape without much timber, down below, a more genial, summery
landscape, gently rising and falling, much planted with elms, and much
of it old grassland upon clay – grassland little disturbed by the ploughing
campaigns of the Second World War. The cliff is chalk – the Lower
Chalk, upon greensand – and is liable to slide and slip; so in between
is a spring, an April landscape, well watered with streams which sidle
out through the greensand, broken up in humps and lumps – the ancient
talus of disintegrated cliff – and well grown with willow and may trees.
Now and then, black in winter against the white chalk, a wood climbs
up the escarpment, a mingling of ash and oak and elder. The cliff does
not run straight, but wriggles in and out, always giving shelter from the
east and sometimes, in the bays of the cliff, from the north winds. In
summer the angle of land immediately below the wall of chalk can glow,
still and breezeless and close. The cliff is marked by a black scattering of
yew trees. An occasional steep water gully cuts from top to bottom, and
many deep tracks go up sideways, joining plain and plain. The sun comes
up abruptly behind the cliff, and sets widely, and as it were, slowly, in the
extent of the wide horizon below. Moonrises have a peculiar excellence, a
full moon sending up a flush above the black velvet of the cliff, over which
it pushes up a yellow rim; then as a full mill-wheel it rides along over the
farms and villages. The nearest towns of any size are eight miles away, the
nearest station three.

In spite of farms and villages below the escarpment, the line of country
has an out-of-the-way look. Tracks and footpaths, but no metalled roads,

run parallel from north-west to south-east. Only a few metalled roads, at wide intervals, cut across the country from clay up to chalk; clay and chalk mingle to a deep, wet mixture, and a number of the farms and hamlets (three or four of them now deserted) lie at the end of tracks which bake hard in summer, and are difficult and dirty under rain. The fox and badger population of the cliff must be considerable. There are badger earths within fifty yards of the farmhouse – disturbed, bare areas of excavation and tunnelling among elders and lean nettles. I once leant over a gate below the cliff in a war summer of tip-and-run raids, when the evening merged into moonlight: with anti-aircraft sparks in the sky, and to the thud and boom of an occasional bomb and the hum of aircraft, I watched the badger come down from its earth, and grub and grunt about under a plum tree, after the ripe yellow plums which lay among the nettles. Nettles – nettles and elder – are dominant plants in this mixture of soils. On the cliff itself one finds harebells and restharrow and clumps of guelder rose; and sometimes patches of sainfoin surviving from past cultivation. A tract of sandy soil under the cliff, not far from the farm, gives a yearly luxuriance of henbane. The damp woods support bluebell, anemone, ramsons, herb Paris. The uneven talus grows fine crops of thistle and ragwort; then, within a hundred yards or so, the flora changes once more. In the damp hayfields on the edge of the farm, the mahogany heads of burnet; field corners with the blue precision of bugle; hemp agrimony and valerian along the wet ditches and drains. It is good fungus country. The elder trees on the cliff are velvet with Jew's Ears; field mushrooms and bluelegs, in great abundance, grow on the chalk plain; and in the occasional plantations of hazel, grown once for the needs of farms, though now little cut except for pea sticks, one can (in a fortunate year) pick baskets of the odd, rubber-sponge-like morel. Foxgloves, disliking lime, are missing throughout the landscape, and are difficult to establish even in gardens. Rosebay willowherb colonies are just, rather late, beginning to establish themselves. There are no adders, but a plenitude of grass snakes, slow-worms and toads. In the past, the lower plain, wet and badly drained, was mosquito-ridden and ague-haunted. The damp decay of the farm buildings and the damp decay of the cliff hangings and their timber still produce an array of mosquitoes, outdoor biters – *Aedes*, and the house-haunting, man-biting *Theobaldia annulata*. But the real pest of the cliff, the chalk, and the talus below the cliff, is the harvest mite, produced every summer in its millions and waiting to crawl onto you from every blade of grass. The clay-dwellers, luckily, are free of its irritation.

The Lower Chalk escarpment stretches one way and the other for miles beyond the limits of the particular sheet of the Ordnance Survey in which the farmhouse stands. But the seven-mile length of the escarpment I am dealing with has its own individualities and character; and there was never a more obvious place for human settlement, once the organisation of life was fairly advanced. Dampness, heaviness of soil, thick wood and undergrowth, and malaria – for the streams over the clay are sluggish – seem to have kept the lower part of the landscape unsettled prehistorically. Along the cliff itself, there is little to be found of early remains, tumuli, traces of cultivation or implements. The Lower Chalk plain gives more evidence of early settlement. Two miles from the clifftop, the Upper Chalk begins with much more abundant traces of man, his tools, his sepulture and his farming.

Under and below the cliff the earliest finds – few enough in number – are in the main Celtic under Roman influence, though some miles along a Roman pavement, probably of the second century, has been uncovered. Then came the Saxons, the ancestors of the present population, the givers of the placenames which still survive. Two or three Saxon cemeteries have been found near the farm, which was itself a Saxon 'tun', conveniently placed where one of the streams comes out beneath the chalk, or rather through the greensand, above the waterproof clay. The position of the villages, the hamlets and the farms has been dictated by the intermittent patches, or platforms, of drier sand, and mainly by the springs from under the cliff, springs which seldom if ever dry up, small springs and large springs. The villages are by the large springs – the largest of which produces two million gallons a day, most of it now used to supply one of the two bigger towns of the district. Two other village springs give some

40,000 gallons a day, and the streams are strong enough to turn a mill within 300 yards of the cliff. It was this water pouring out into the mire of the clay plain which must have differentiated the cliff and the clay areas even more strongly than they are differentiated now. The Saxon 'tuns' lie along the cliff, the 'tun on the river Worf' (now a large village and known still earlier as Ellendune – 'Elder-tree-down'), 'Cilia's tun', 'Dung tun', 'Ash tree tun', 'Neat [Cattle] tun' (now a village), 'Bubbe's tun', 'the tun by the gap' (a gap through the cliff). Just below, on the wet clay, are few tuns and many names of marsh and wood, or poor settlements: 'cottage marsh', 'the marsh', 'thorn hill', 'reed-lands', 'midge corner', 'thick thorn', 'cottage place', the farm of 'Adam at the braec' – which means land newly cultivated. There are five or six of these 'braec' names on the clay within the seven miles. For this settling within the comfort and shelter of the cliff there were psychological as well as practical reasons. Running water is not only drink, but life. To be perched above the plain is to free the spirit from gloom as well as the feet from mud. The wife of one of the recent tenants of the farm, a rather shy, secretive woman, was dismal at the prospect of moving down to a farmhouse on the clay. She would feel, she said, the loss of the hill at her back and the loss of the wide view from her windows and garden – a view which stretches around like the countryside in Rubens' landscape of the Château de Steen in the National Gallery. In fact, the Saxon settlers – probably, in this part of England, rather late settlers between AD 550 and 600 – had every reason for pleasure and satisfaction. Mosquitoes were nothing out of the way. On the talus of the cliff and below they had pastures, on the cliff itself and down in the marshes timber for houses and firing, up on the Lower Chalk, flat, excellent cornland.

Today the farms still straddle the cliff, cornland above, cow grounds and hayfields below, and the depth of the tracks joining the two indicates centuries of farm traffic. A very few Celtic names remain within the seven miles, and probably there was some mingling of the old and the new inhabitants; but the kinsmen living together in the new tuns settled the future and the organisation of the district for 1300 years ahead of them.

The farm of this book was one such 'tun'; it still has its Saxon name of the

'Ash tree Tun', Ashton, or Ashton Farm, and alongside it is the 'Neat Tun', the Cattle Tun, or Netton. The Neat Tun has developed through the ages into a village. The Ash tree Tun has declined from a very small village or hamlet, simply into a farm, along with one cottage in repair, one in ruins, and the foundations of a few more. One must picture the original tun, in either case, as a small collection of wattle-and-daub, thatched dwellings, whose inhabitants held the land in common. The modern village of the Cattle Tun only gained its church and its schoolhouse and its parochial status within the last hundred years or so; the existing parish was carved out of two other parishes, partly because of the poverty and backwardness of its people. Everything that William Marshall or Arthur Young says of country roads in their agricultural surveys of the eighteenth century was true of this neighbourhood. For more than a thousand years, Neat and Ash tree Tuns had lived a self-sufficient, more or less self-subsisting life under their cliff, cut off by roads which were conduits of winter mud. The roads are now metalled – save for the track into Ashton Farm and some of the entrance ways into other farms; there is a bus service, and men who go by bus or else cycle to factory work in the town live out here in the council houses; but as late as 1918 it was impossible in winter to drive a motorcycle the three miles into the station. A jaundiced and unhappy clergyman's wife wrote this in 1904, of the next village: 'There are two roads possible for us inhabitants of Snorum End, one along the high-road, … one up the so-called 'street' of the village. But even these two avenues are not always open. After a day's rain, the whole place is transformed into a quagmire of whitey-grey, clogging, clinging mud, which is unconscionably slow a-drying. The use of a bicycle for four months of the year is out of the question, and a drive is a luxury not to be contemplated. Thus it comes about that through the winter we never go out of the place, and often, for months together, we see no single face from the world outside.'

'No face from outside' must have been roughly true of this district from 600 to 1920. The clerical reformers of the 1840s, when church and church-school were founded, spoke feelingly and piously of the immorality, poverty and quarrelsomeness of the people of the Neat Tun, who had a taste for incest and other behaviours. The changes since 1904, since 1918, are startling enough. Not everyone speaks with the same accent in the village. Not all the farmers belong to the district: one is from Somerset, another from Shropshire. A schoolmistress speaks Derbyshire, a trade unionist in a council house speaks Lancashire. They listen to the *Brains Trust, Saturday Night Theatre* and *Jane Eyre* (which they have never read). They have electricity; and will soon have drainage, and sometime or other a big measure of modern housing; yet even now one can well see why the neighbouring parson's wife called her book *A Modern Boeotia*, and quoted on her title page '*Bos tibi, Phoebus ait, solis occurret in agris*'; and also why John Aubrey of the seventeenth century wrote of the people hereabouts, that 'the Indigenae, or Aborigines, speake drawling; they are phlegmatique, skins pale and livid, slow and dull, heavy of spirit', that they are 'melancholy, contemplative, and malicious', fond of lawsuits, 'more apt to be fanatiques; their persons are generally plump and feggy; gallipot eies, and some black; but they are generally handsome enough. It is a woodsere country, abounding much with sowre and austere plants, as sorrel etc, which makes their humours sowre, and fixes their spirit'. And he adds that in one hundred, in these 'wett clayy parts', 'there have ever been reputed witches'.

Improvement or no, some trace of the causes of the old anathemas of 1675 and 1904 still remains, owing in part to a slower development here than in some other districts, districts even of the same county, and in part to a rural social decay which has gone on alongside plenty of material betterment. The spirit of the village community has weakened; there is little sympathy between farmer and worker. Agriculturally, the old system of the open fields, which began with the tuns, lasted here late, until the 1820s. The Board of Agriculture's reporter in 1794 spoke of the water-logged common fields in the 'deep, cold vein of land' around the village, which needed to be drained, turned into pasture and enclosed; he spoke of the badness of the roads, the very miserable state of the labourers – the few labourers, because 'little manual labour' was 'done to the unenclosed land'. One may well think now that another revolution, scientific and social, is needed in local agriculture, if one looks at the state of the farms, the farm buildings and the leaking, squalid, tied houses of the farmworkers.

To go back from the Neat Tun to the Ash tree Tun. The Ash tree Tun lies a quarter of a mile across the fields; and was reached until some ten years ago by a difficult track, beginning off the main metalled road, halfway up the cliff. The track was steep at the first, and slippery; then a trough of mud when it reached the flat and ran along under the cliff and beneath a wood (the wood where I watched the badger under the plum tree). A big step to bringing the farm into the world was the purchase of a large, long field directly between the village and the farm, through which an open, less miry track leads straight from road to farmyard. The old track – the thousand-year-old track – sufficed until the coming of lorry and motorcar. The Ash tree Tun was once, and originally, a hamlet. As I have said, the still discernible layout of the hamlet gives one some notion of its first arrangement of Saxon wattle-and-daub hutments. The farmhouse stands some fifty yards from the base of the cliff. The cottages were – the two still are – tucked closer to the cliff, in two groups along the track to left and right. The group beyond the farmhouse continued until 1870. The gault clay under the greensand, which in turn lies under the chalk, has a sluggish habit, in the words of the Geological Survey memoir, of flowing; and it is this, every so often, which causes a founder, a tumbling of the cliff. Such a founder happened in the night, in 1870. The cliff came tumbling down; masses of greensand and chunks of the hard, blocky chalk rollocked on to the cottages, twisted and tilted them. Some of the people – no one was killed – had to scramble out through the bedroom windows, including a bedridden old woman. Now, the last stumps of the cottages have disappeared, the overgrown gardens survive, a few plum trees, and some gooseberry bushes – plums and gooseberries still bear well after 76 years – and a trace or two of the stone pathways in from the track. Fragments of blue china, brown glazed earthenware and glass lie about under the elder bushes; and I found there once a rusted sickle, thin-bladed, of the shape which survives on the Soviet flag – the sickle used for reaping of wheat and barley on the 'white lands' above. A minor slip ruined one cottage in

A wall of sarsen blocks used with brick.

the other cluster, nearer the farm. One cottage remains in repair, rebuilt by weekenders (rare in this neighbourhood) when it was upon the edge of absolute decay. So the tun settlement of the sixth century has dwindled now after 1300 years to the farmer and his family, still drawing (though now it is piped indoors) their water from the original, causative spring.

South-west of the farm and village, further along the cliff, the 'tuns' have much the same nature. One has developed into a village, one into a hamlet. Another ('Bubbe's tun'), reached only by a steep track over the cliff or a long mud lane from a firm road which rides across the clay, has been deserted within the last ten years; its buildings have collapsed, the roof timbers have fallen in, and only the chimneys (it is – or was – mainly a seventeenth- and eighteenth-century building) survive out of the mess of beam and masonry. On one chimney two insulators and a foot or two of telephone wire speak of the farm's brief linking with the world outside itself. The doctor's stories of reaching this farmhouse at midnight, in storms of wind and rain, riding on a pony and guided by a storm-lantern, drive into one a realisation of life upon such an unapproachable site, as it was in the earlier centuries. Yet this farmstead, one feels even now in its sprawl, its nearness to extinction, has been thoroughly humanised, is a place, a wide platform in the sun, protected by the cliff, open southward and westward to the horizon, on which, other things being equal, one would naturally choose to be born, to live, to die. Both this and the farm, or tun, next to it, have lost their white lands (ie 'wheat lands') up above, one through sale (which is true also of the Ash tree Tun of this book), the other through the war and the building of an aerodrome. Their deep tracks up over the cliff, now never used, will soon fill up with thistles, then nettles and then the inevitable elder trees. A barn, conveniently placed at the foot of the gap to the upper land, and well above the farmstead itself, has been allowed to fall in; and the second of these farmsteads, the one named the Tun by the 'Corf' or gap (dryly situated on a platform of reddish greensand some 200 yards from the cliff), is falling apart stone by stone, beam by beam – all save the dwelling-house. The cows are milked in a windy, decaying range of stalls, the horses are stabled under a thatch roof, which has half fallen away, and which grows a crop of raspberry canes on the other half; and even the elm trees around the yard are slowly dying. In ten years perhaps all the buildings will be flat.* Yet this farm is fortunate in having a narrow public road to its gateway, serving the farm and the few cottages gathered below.

In between these two farms and Netton and Ashton Farm stands Littletown, the one parochial village under the cliff, with an early church, a manor house alongside still in the hands of a family which has owned it for some generations, a vicarage, occupied for the best part of a century by father and son-in-law, and a public house, whose signboard bears the arms of the manor house family. Decay here is rather less pronounced, and the society rather more closely knit. The parish and village are still articulated by the backbone of an older society. Out of the past of the Saxons and the Normans, the manorial system, the enclosures, the social and agricultural revolution, has grown in this village something more viable and stable than one can find anywhere else in the seven miles, where the cliff and the social structure seem to be crumbling together; though it would be fairer to say that the structure crumbles and rebuilds itself as well, if in differential degrees and at a differential rate.

* Sooner than ten years. I wrote this in the autumn; going to the farm again in early summer, I found the remains of the barn, in which the horses were stabled, scattered among nettles.

The framework of a decayed barn still firm despite the lack of roof.

THE TUNS

WHAT THIS BOOK will dwell most upon is the actual substance and the appearance, in detail, of the farmhouse and its buildings, and surroundings. But something more needs to be said upon how the farms developed and grew. Only a few of them – and Ashton Farm is not one – were Domesday Book manors. They all lie within the same hundred, the subdivision of the shire; and the traditional meeting place of this hundred, about halfway in the seven-mile length, was not far below the cliff in the parish I have mentioned with its manor house and church. Some of the farms, continuing the pattern of mediaeval organisation, are grouped together in villages. Four farmsteads with yards and buildings lie close together, for instance, in a quarter of a mile of road, in Netton. Around them and above the cliff were the open fields, which the farmers cultivated in strips and on which they fed their swine, their cattle and their sheep under the communal herdsmen and shepherds. One farm, the Manor farm, stands back a little from the group, down a short lane, and was demesne land, no doubt enclosed and cultivated separately from the common fields at an early date. Just below this farm was the manorial mill, used until within memory. Half of the iron framework of the wheel was salvaged during the Second World War, half still lies in the pit. On another of the manors, which has no stream strong enough to turn a wheel, the farmers were served by a windmill, memory of which remains only in the placename of Windmill Hill. Miserable and with their soil impoverished, the common fields, the bulk of the manor, continued in the old rotation of crops until, as I have said, just over a hundred years ago, when an enclosure act put an end to the past. But the farms – most of them small, even as small as thirty-five and forty acres – were not all compactly assembled. Some included 'white land' up above, some have boundaries running into each other; and it is a reminder of the past that cows must be driven up the road from yards to fields at some distance away, mucking and muddying the hard surface and the margins in winter. Other farms are outliers either of Netton manor or another of the manors, separated from the common lands and enclosed early on, early consolidated holdings, which only lately have ceased to be the property of large-scale landowners, whose estates have been split up and sold; and to that, partly, to the agricultural depression in the 1880s, which brought re-equipment to a standstill, and to the small capitalisation of the individual farmers, is due the fact that the out-of-date farm buildings are steadily decaying. On the old marsh lands, the old wastes of the various manors, were a good many isolated cottages, many of which have disappeared but for orchard plots and boundaries and a fragment or two of willow pattern or the earthenware of pitchers by the streams from which the cottagers drew their water. The intricate series of little-used field paths, by which many of these isolated cottages were served, are now marked more clearly on the map than on the ground. A few oaken 'squeeze-bellies', the stiles which are made of two uprights set close together so that cattle cannot pass through, survive on these paths. An Ordnance Map of 1828 shows them not as paths at all, but as roads or unfenced tracks. One of these cottages was in the middle of a wood which comes down the cliff and spreads along the further slope of the talus. Much of it was standing ten years ago, under a fine tall clump of white lilac, and with an enormous apple tree nearby. The last tenant was a gamekeeper, who lived on there by himself, keeping his pigs, or a pig, in a natural sty formed by a hollow tree. When he was moved in his old age from the wood to a village, he complained of the 'silence' and 'loneliness' of his new home. After ten years, this chalk cottage has soaked and sunk into a mound. Here again the gooseberry bushes survive, with the lilac and the apple tree, as well as a few persistent clumps of snowdrops and monkshood.

Most of the farms whose names end in -ton can be traced back to the Domesday Book or to deeds of the thirteenth century. The land under the escarpment to the south-west is not so clayey and low-lying as the land below Netton and Ashton, and rises slightly over rocky Corallian beds; it was easier land to settle, and many of the names on it go back at least to the twelfth and eleventh centuries and even beyond. On the clay lands, many of the farms date only from the eighteenth century, and particularly the last thirty years of the century, years of farming advance and new, improved methods of tillage. Long as it was before Netton and its neighbouring, still more ancient manor were enclosed, the older manor came in the seventeenth century into the hands of an Oxford college, still the chief landlord of the district; and college ownership gave some fillip to the draining and to the taking-in and enclosing of new farms.

The farmhouse of Ashton Farm itself and of most of its neighbours under the protection of the cliff are much alike in plan, in material and in age. The bulk of the house belongs to the seventeenth century – the buildings around are later, as we shall see. A stone let in to one chimney is carved with the initials 'RS' and the year 1668; but that is deceptive. Many, indeed most, of the houses on the earlier farms seem to have been rebuilt late in the seventeenth century (perhaps 'refashioned' would be the better word), in the period of new confidence and settlement after the Civil War and the end of the Commonwealth – rebuilt or refashioned, around an older core of sixteenth-century date. To quote William Harrison's *Description of England*, published in 1577 (and quoted by Lord Ernle), every man turned builder in those years and 'pulled down the olde house and set up a new after his owne devise', for it was a prosperous agricultural time, when prices were high and when farmers became wealthy. Lord Ernle quotes also from William Webb writing in 1621 of the yeomen of another county: 'In building and furniture of their houses, till of late years, they used the old manner of the Saxons; for they had their fire in the midst of the house against a hob of clay, and their oxen also under the same roof; but within these forty years it is altogether altered, so that they have built chimnies, and furnished other parts of their houses accordingly.' And it is just these chimneys, in their massive lower structure, with their enormous fireplaces, which have survived in the farmhouses of this district, with additions around them of a hundred years later. In the eighteenth century, porches were often added – as at Ashton Farm – and just after the mid-nineteenth century, in the prosperity of Victorian farming, often a new wing was tacked on. But outwardly, the impression is one of the seventeenth century; though a variety of circumstances, the availability of materials, the isolation of the district, and the fact that the prosperity of the farmers, even in well-to-do times, was never likely to have been of the higher, or highest, orders, have made the houses serviceable and homely, and Boeotian, rather than elegant; and have kept them, as farmhouses go in an open country, on the small side.

As for the buildings around them, there is some conflict of evidence among the agricultural reporters of the eighteenth century, who generalise about a much wider area. Further away from the cliff, the farming was mainly based upon cow-keeping, the fattening of calves, and the supply of an excellent cheese to the local factors who bought for the London market (one of the local farms is named Cowage Farm, *Cowic*, in the Domesday Book, meaning 'Cow dairy farm'); and one reporter, William Marshall (1789), having the cheese-making in his mind, and the typical dairy farm, talks of the houses being near the centre of the farms, with large cow-grounds reaching up to the yards which are 'in general, mere milking yards; without any shelter, for cattle, in winter'. And he wrote of areas in which 'few traces of common field are at present evident'. If one goes only a mile or two from the cliff, on to clay land which has been predominantly pasture or poor, waterlogged arable, one sees the truth of his statement; the range of buildings is mean and scanty even now, without large barns; and with modern cowsheds. But here the position was different. Pasturage and cows were important (witness Netton or Neat Tun: Cattle Tun), and cheese-making became important, but both the later maintenance of the open fields below the cliff, which were partly under the plough, and the 'white lands' above, cropped with corn, demanded more than mere milking yards. Thomas Davis, reporting on the county

in 1794, visited this very district along the cliff; but he contents himself
with saying that the layout of the farms was much what it was in the
southern part of the county, on the wider, more open lands. There, the
farms usually had 'three barns, or at least three threshing floors ... to
avoid mixing different kinds of corn; and a barn on stone pillars to keep
out rats and mice, for wheat; stabling for horses, a cowshed for cattle
wintered in the yard on straw; a granary, pigsties, a drinking pool'. That
layout seems roughly true of the farms under the cliff, though not many
of them were large enough to run to a multiplicity of barns; and few – I
only know one – of the large barns built on stilts now survive. Ashton
Farm has its stilted granary, pigsties, a double range of cowsheds and a
waggon shed, the modern addition of a galvanised Dutch barn, all around
its one vast thatched barn, which has the stabling for horses at the far end.
(Thomas Davis also remarked that few oxen were used hereabouts by the
farmers, who preferred horses.) Stalls for fattening calves stood just below
the yard, but have now long tumbled down.

Farm buildings, into which more wood enters than stone, have not the
durability of the farmhouses, nor is there the same personal incentive to
keep them in repair. Judging from appearances, few of the buildings on
Ashton Farm and the other cliff farms are more than 150 or 200 years old.
Many of them are nineteenth-century, built in the great farming period of
1840 to 1880, built particularly in this neighbourhood towards the end of
that period, when cheese-making gave way to milk.

The last of Bubbe's Tun. The great central chimney of chalk above the bedroom.

THE FARM AT PRESENT

BEFORE THE LAST WAR, the arable land of the farms grew more
thistles than corn. Cow-keeping and bullocks, milk for the local
milk factory – so the order of things was mainly composed. Hay and
a small amount of root crops and dredge corn made up the farming, in
the real sense of farming. Imported cattle-cake was a mainstay. Some
of the farms, I remarked, have now lost their 'white lands'; one will see
on them no more the sight of waggonloads of corn coming down the
ancient cliff tracks behind horses or tractor. The tracks are fenced off at
top and bottom, and have pathetically lost their purpose. Ashton, like
the other scattered farms – the farms not grouped together in a village –
stands, house and buildings, on a nearly level platform, at a wide angle
to the cliff. The cow-grounds come up to the yard; the hay meadows are
further off on the flat, concealed by tall rows of elm. Beyond the yard
and the barn, an orchard of old, cankered trees, which still produce a
good harvest of apples in a kind season, slopes gently up towards one
of the cottages. It includes a pear tree or two, and a couple of walnut
trees. Modern, fat daffodils (rather ugly ones) have been planted through
the orchard; but their place is taken later on by nettles, which have to
be scythed away before the apples begin to drop. A plum tree or two,
some of old varieties not often marketed or purchasable now (the waxy,

beautiful Blaisdon Red, for instance), gooseberry bushes which produce small, hairy fruit, and a few red currants and black currants, and a couple of wall pears against the farmhouse itself, complete the rather neglected fruits of the farm. Neither time, care nor money have been spent on them. The apple trees are not even banded in the autumn. If late frosts hold away, if the trees and bushes bear fruit, well and good: if not, wait until next year. Quinces and medlars grow only on one of the farms – not at Ashton – and neither is picked. The flower gardens, too, show evidence of having been better tilled in the past, with more care and fancy. Many of the farm gardens have a long south wall of red brick, sometimes ornamentally or carefully built, the path bordered by dwarf box. But most often what flowers there are, around the houses or in the gardens – everlasting pea, leopard's bane, lilies of the valley, a few roses, Solomon's seal, woodruff, a clump of peonies or Christmas roses – live more upon sufferance than attention. Small families, perhaps only a son and a daughter, with little outside labour, male or female, mean that the farmer's wife has few minutes of leisure in the week, and little surplus energy to attend to the flowers. If she takes time off, it is for a motor ride, or a visit to the cinema, combined with shopping – and reasonably enough. At Ashton Farm the peonies flourish and get a few spadefuls of dung, since they are six feet precisely from the yard; and being rose-scented peonies, they deserve it. The others are not so fortunate: the most they get is occasional dung, and a little incomplete weeding, which at least keeps down the couch grass.

The impression the farm gives is of a life in many ways more convenient, with water piped in, bathroom, modern grates, Aga cooker and so on, in many ways more convenient, in many ways easier; but much less gracious, less integrated than it may well have been in the past. The pride of gardening, for instance, now belongs to the cottage people, down in the village – not to the farmers' wives, not to the farmworkers, who grow food on their allotment ground, and neglect the gardens of their farm-tied cottages, but to the trade unionists, who work in the town, live in council houses, have a security of tenure, and a recreative delight in flowers.

These new gardeners plant a good many of the newer flowers of the large-scale commercial seed-growers, and do not merely continue to grow the older flowers of farm or cottage garden. This is a change in itself that one can look at in two ways, or three. It breaks a tradition; it breaks an old local uniformity, and in doing so it begins to impose a new universal uniformity, like the uniformity of the styles of the council houses which arise out of the flowerbeds. Since the change has not been completed, one can still see something of the older local sameness in flowers. One of the village farmhouses has a biggish garden, in which, till recently, flowers were better tended than in most of the farmhouse gardens; mainly because the farmer, who enjoyed gardening, had given up his farm, letting the fifty acres but keeping on the house in his retirement. In cottage garden after garden all around are repeated particular species and varieties which still grow in the farm garden – everlasting pea, for instance, a particular variety of the ox-eye daisy, woodruff, caper spurge and double soapwort.

On the farms, life and the amenities given in the past seem, at the best, to be held; not so much is added, little is renewed, much is patched, much is slipping away, decaying, vanishing. The eighteenth-century porch at Ashton Farm, a heavy affair of timber and lead, supported on round pillars of oak, fell down. It was removed, the pillars were sold, and the house remained porchless. Much else, which still had a daily use, has fallen down, and also been removed, not rebuilt. In 1864, a now forgotten tenant of one of the cliff farms cut a white horse in the cliff directly above his own chimneys, eighty-six feet long by sixty-one feet high. But the horse today is shabby; it is years since any tenant or owner interested himself in its grooming.

Strongly one feels that an old life is dead, a species of new half-life struggles on, fortified with certain fossils of opinion adopted from the past, and that a new life cannot develop decisively without some upheaval of ideas, practice and organisation. The existing half-life is an analogue of the church at morning service, with three people, the vicar and the vicar's wife. Of the farm under the cliff now actually deserted, now actually ruined, where a line of occupation going back to the

thirteenth century and beyond has now been ended for ever, I have felt
that melancholy:

> Once smoothly, smoothly curved this meadow
> Where the lumps of nettle lay their shadow
> And the rabbits side-step to the round-flowered
> Elders, under the tall long wall of leaves:
>
> Sheep in their antique attitude hump in
> The gateway. Thatch thins under the elder,
> Daws chuckle; and the bile-green yews, swished
> By the mournful summer winds, continue.
>
> He lies in stone who once was owner;
> In a book on place-names an earlier dweller;
> In unread herd-lists, who built the dung-splashed
> Drawing-room; successful these,
>
> Authentic; place-name, and yews, the rose
> Remain; but history took the place
> For dead, and looked and left; even the rats of progress went
> And honest thistles grew.

And I may as well quote, since it comes from the same source of
under-the-cliff melancholia, another poem, of the defeat of the seasons
among these farms:

> This is when the scarlet lords-and-ladies
> Glitter erect in the wet angle of the hedges
> And shrivel soon,
>
> And again the bland leaves curl and colour,
> Seeds are black in their deep sockets, and another
> Shrivelling moon
>
> Half-lights the calmer times of indecision,
> Rain damps down the summer's middle-class ambition,
> And very soon
>
> A stale and unconvinced denial of defeat
> Mutters with pauses from the elder hedge its weak
> Self-pitying tune:
>
> Toads pause, the handsome slugs will hide
> And the caught bee dry and fade inside
> The emptied room.

I shall have something more to add in detail, in a chapter on ruins. On this particular ruined farm, even if the rats have left, two human associates remain, a pair of white owls, barn owls, who occupy the upper chamber of the weatherboarded granary – a building which has slipped off its stones and tilted forwards, but which was so well constructed that it still holds firmly together. If an eighteenth-century tenant of this farm were to come back, he would find a good many changes here even in the birds of the cliff district. The jackdaws he would find as abundant as ever, nesting in holes among the block chalk, where the sloping escarpment turns into an actual, ivy- and root-grown cliff; he would see them again planing and volplaning and hovering up on the upward currents of air which rise against the slope. Green woodpeckers, sliding and dipping and rising in flight along the meadows, he would still see every day. But the white owl population is down. In summer, too, there is only an occasional pair of quails or corncrakes. A lane with the Middle English name of Cock Road (a common name in the county for a lane where woodcock were caught in nets) suggests that in days when the clay lands were marshier – as in the eighteenth-century – and there was more wood on the cliff, woodcock were much less common than they are now. Coming back, the farmer would certainly be puzzled by the day-long melancholy calling of little owls from the meadows around and below his farm – from the meadows, in fact, all along the cliff.

The farmer would find bile-green yews still flourishing around the farm, but their function as a windbreak scarcely realised. His modern successors know only that the yew leaves are poisonous to their cows and horses; that occasional branches of yew make good, durable posts. They fence the yew trees off from the stock, and would willingly cut them down, if it was not that yews are large and tough and obstinate. In the landscape, the yews are an element beyond their numbers, a darkness against the pale green, or according to the season, the pale yellow of the cliff, whose slopes are scored by the cattle into terraces. At Ashton Farm someone once planted a line of yews up and down the slope, from the cliff-track above the farm buildings to the summit. They are well grown, healthy and deep-rooted into the chalk, and carefully fenced off. Elders grow along this dark line of yews, to about a third of their height. At right angles to the yews, along the track before it begins to ascend, a later tenant planted a row of limes, which have the comfortable, roundish shape of corn-stacks (perhaps for his bees, though in ten years I have never seen these limes in flower, maybe because of the aphis and the honey-dew. Part of the cliff a mile or two away was given the Saxon name 'beona cnoll' – bees' hill – now pronounced Bynol). Below the limes, and close above the farm itself, stands a company of elms, a bit thinned by disease, whose tops come about level with the lime-tree row. Seen in April, these trees above the farm, and on the cliff, make a pattern of tones and colours. The cliff-slopes themselves a yellow-green, with patches of chalk showing through; the yews almost black, the new leaves of the elders underneath a green, light and clear. The elms, just in leaf, of a green still lighter, and then in between, still bare, the compact branchiness, the reddish, gleaming brown of the lime trees. The scene, with the farm below, a complex of thatch, of galvanised iron and stone tiles, has the most serene, comfortable look of human composition; looking at the farm in this way from above, particularly in an evening light, part direct, part reflected from the cliff, or coming up to it in sunlight across cow-ground, one can well believe in a thousand years, and more, of human occupation and modification; one can feel the affection which generation after generation must have felt for this cliff-land; an affection which matured slowly, which depended upon secure tenure and upon time for its growth. Like vicarages, Ashton Farm has probably had more tenants since 1900 than for the 200 years before. It is held now to be a young man's farm, a farm to be rid of for plainer and milder surroundings on a hard road by or before early middle age.

I have said little or nothing yet about the actual substance and appearance of the farmhouse and its buildings, or the substance and appearance of its neighbours – beyond mentioning a seventeenth-century date, and tile, thatch and galvanised. Thatch is the earliest, authentic roof-covering of the district, and has been so, of course, from the Saxon settlement down to our own day; Ashton Farm has thatch and tile – stone tile – on the farmhouse roof, thatch on the big barn and the waggon-shed, galvanised on the Dutch barn, and galvanised replacing thatch on the shippens – the cowsheds. The barn makes one side of the square, the shippens two more sides, while half of the fourth side is filled in with the dwelling-house and its garden wall. Piped out of the ground in one corner, and pouring into a pond, is the foundation spring of Ashton Farm – a part of it, since much of the flow is now taken indoors. The waste from the spring soaked away, until a few years back, into the centre of the yard. Add to the spring the passage of waggon and cart, the tramplings of cattle and horses, and more water in the form of an occasional rain torrent pouring down the track, as down a watercourse, from the flat lands overhead – and the yard in January became a basin of viscous mud, deepening towards the centre, in which one could have drowned a sheep or a calf. Only a blessed frost hardened and cleaned it up – until one previous farmer could stand it no more, hired a concrete-mixer from the town and squared off ninety per cent of the yard in neat solidity (leaving the other ten per cent unconcreted was in spiritual character; so perhaps was patching up a few of the shaky brick walls with surplus concrete).

Looking at the walls of the house and the buildings, three materials, roofing apart, at once speak to the eye: timber, in the form of weatherboarding, chalk and brick, though that is not everything. Look at the footings of the barn and the older shippens and the garden wall, and you see stone – a knobbly, reddish-brown stone. Behind the lilies of the valley and the stunted, starved veronica bushes in the flowerbed along the wall of the house, chunks of this same stone – which is sarsen from the downs – lie deep in the ground under the lowest blocks of chalk. One building, or part of it, happens to be made of a hard, greyish-yellow stone, not unlike the familiar oolitic limestones of the Cotswold farms and barns. But for reasons we shall see, little enough of this stone has been used under the cliff, except at the south-western end of our district. Timber, sarsen, chalk, brick, this harder limestone – all were local.

Ease of transport has now ended the dependence of local architecture upon the local geological formations. What new buildings there are

hereabouts – for instance, the older council houses (and it will apply to
the new council houses, now being built in the wrong place, without any
regard to the village as a social structure, which has taken a thousand years
or more to grow) – contain little or nothing produced within forty miles.
Bricks from the London area, slates from Wales, timber from Archangel.
If the newer buildings do not fit too well into the village, it is, all the same,
less the fault of the materials than of elevation and design. Their colour is
not always disagreeable; their shape, bad enough in itself, is absolutely at
variance with that of the houses of an older date, which happen to be local
in their substance. 'The style of a national architecture', Ruskin wrote in
Stones of Venice, 'may evidently depend, in a great measure, upon the
nature of the rocks of the country', a remark quoted by J. A. Howe in his
excellent *Geology of Building Stones* to introduce the correspondence of
geological formation and architecture in the English country districts; and
much irrational sentiment in these days of preservation, adulation of the
past, and contempt of the possibilities of the present, has been raised upon
Ruskin's observation, upon that preaching elaborated by Ruskin out of
his early exploration of the buildings in Cumberland, his early reading of
Wordsworth's *Guide to the Lakes*. If, of course, you employ a hard stone
which is not too easy to cut, your house will be liable to take upon itself a
simple shape. If a district style has evolved, in which that stone is used, and
the style is alive, buildings in a group will have a homogeneity within which
plenty of variation occurs. There is a practical connection between local
building stone and the seemliness of houses; rather than an irrational and
semi-mystical one. Ruskin realised that, if some of our modern preservers
do not. 'The uncultivated mountaineer of Cumberland', he wrote, 'has no
taste and no idea of what architecture means. He never thinks of what
is right and what is beautiful, but he builds what is most adapted to his
purpose and most easily erected; by suiting the building to the use of his
own life he gives it humility, and by raising it with the nearest material
adapts it to his situation.' Which is not saying quite enough. An idiom, a
style, a vernacular idiom or vernacular style, if you like, does grow up,
which is taste, and is an idea of architecture; and if that vernacular style

dies, monstrosities can be built no less from the beds of a local quarry than of bricks from some Hertfordshire brick-kiln. The stone may be less amenable to uglinesses of shape. If stone is used, its colour may be cool and sombre, whereas bricks from outside may be over-regular, smooth and strident. These cool and sombre tones may not be very different from the local tones of the soil; but one is apt to see more soil than original rock, and more green of grass and vegetation than soil. In Cumberland it may be another matter. Use of the nearest material, where so much rock is visible, may adapt a house to its situation. But elsewhere? In the lowlands? Well, first, the vernacular idiom has gone, is dead. It can only be faked, and often it is faked with obedience to Ruskin upon local stone; and with horrible results. And second, there is another reason why buildings, even of local stone, are often adapted ill to their site. In many parts of England, buildings of the last twenty years, none too ill-shaped out of the local stone which has been predominantly used, are inharmonious and raw, and attract too much unwilling attention to themselves – simply because they are naked, naked of trees and shrubs.

One sees new farms, new houses, new cottages, around which no one has thought to plant a tree. Rather than the use of outside, alien, factory-made materials, and poor copybook design, the death of the inclination to plant is responsible for very much of the ugliness of architecture in the landscape. More encouragement of planting, less talk and regret over the use of local materials, would remedy much of the rawness and unpleasantness; and while talking of the poor hold upon the graces of life and their continuance on the farm, I might have mentioned that few of the farmers have ever planted a tree – unless it be a plum or an apple or a buddleia – in their lives. The yews, the limes, the elms, the walnuts around the farm vary in age from two hundred years or more for the yew trees to forty or a hundred for the rest. Somewhere about 1910, to judge from their size, a tenant planted the small grove of larches alongside the track from the farm to the cottages and the main road, to give himself a supply of fencing-posts. At some time, willows were planted for use in thatching, and a patch of hazels on the cliff for hurdling and various odds and ends.

But that is all. The farmers have never planted in late years, but have never been backward in cutting and destroying; and sooner or later the face of the landscape will tell the difference.

As for the building materials, the substance of the farm, all from tiles to timber, were, as I say, more or less autochthonous. The use of the two of them, the chalk and the sarsen, demanded the evolution of a traditional, local technique (which has died out: the use of chalk and sarsen was closely mingled); and all of them need a section or a chapter to themselves. Chalk was the most important, the one nearest to hand, and easiest to quarry. But since the base was often of sarsen stone, one may as well begin at the bottom.

SARSEN STONES

A PART FROM CHURCHES, I do not know any house immediately around Ashton Farm older in date than the sixteenth century. The houses of the Englishmen on the land continued to be made mainly of wood until the end of that century, when the stone farmhouses with their massive main chimneys began to go up, and the countryside began to look, architecturally, much as it does still. In fact, the chimney, with its great hearth, and a side oven (now bricked in) survives in Ashton farmhouse, from somewhere around 1570 or 1580. It is a chalk chimney, capped with brick in later times; and the seventeenth-century chalk walls of the house are laid upon tougher foundations of undressed sarsen stone, which retains its original reddish rind, polished by erosion and weather. Sarsens are sandstone. They are the weathered fragments of the crust, united and hardened by silica, of old beds of sand which once lay above the chalk. For the most part, under their growth of lichen, they have that reddish colour. Inside, when they are split, the sarsens show a clean, glistening white.

Of their use in local building there is written, as well as actual, evidence as early as the period of the Civil Wars. Yet sarsens were, not unnaturally, the primeval building substance of the locality. Up on the downs, where they lie, grey and rough with lichen, eight burial chambers (of which five are left) were made of sarsen blocks. Sarsen was used for the making of Avebury, and a mile or two from the farmhouse a small stone circle, or rather double circle, of sarsen stones stood in a field on the wheat lands. The circle has fallen now, most of the stones have vanished, and only a few are visible above the grass. Next, sarsens occur in the walls and the foundations of the churches. To the medieval church-builders, or to the builders of the sixteenth-century farmhouses, it is, I agree, a pretty long step from Avebury and the early Bronze Age.

But the sarsens lay up there on the downs to be used, lay where nothing else was at once to hand save flint and friable chalk. It was just the obvious material to take at different ages, when different building needs arose.

The first man to mention sarsens either by their old name of 'Saracen stones' or as 'Grey Wethers' – the grey sheep of stone lying in flocks upon, and in, the downland turf – was Richard Symonds, the Civil War soldier, in his diary of jottings (mainly about tombs and coats of arms in country churches). He wrote of one of the villages above the cliff that it was 'a place so full of grey pibble stones of great bignes as is not usually seene; they breake them and build their houses of them and walls, laying mosse betweene, the inhabitants call them Saracens stones, and in this parish, a mile and a halfe in length, they lie so thick as you may go upon them all the way. They call that place the Grey Wethers, because afar off they looke like a flock of Sheepe.' The name 'Saracen stones' – a derivation of the modern sarsen which the *Oxford English Dictionary* is inclined to accept – was a tribute to their mysteriousness, a tribute, I would say, as much to their isolated, obvious presence on the downs as to their use in the megalithic structures. 'Saracen's stones' has its parallel in such expressions as Saracen's Corn or Saracen's Soap, or in the Saracen's Head given as a name to public houses. 'Sarsenry' was an early name for the Saracen people. The borough accounts of a downland town show that stones which must have been sarsens were being used to repair the Grammar School wall many years before the Civil Wars, in fact in 1575. John Aubrey is the next witness in the mid-seventeenth century, commenting on the use of sarsens in the Avebury 'temple': 'I have heard the minister of Aubury say those huge stones may be broken in what part of them you please without any great trouble. The manner is thus: they make a fire on that line of the stone where they would have it to crack; and, after the stone is well heated, draw over a line with cold water, and immediately give a smart

Sarsen. Rough paving of sarsen blocks in the farmyard.

knock with a smyth's sledge, and it will break like the collets at the glasse house.' Aubrey's editor talks of the same 'system of destruction' being used in his time, round about 1800, both on the sarsens up on the downs and in the Circle. The other writer and antiquary to comment with bitterness upon their employment in local building was William Stukeley, writing of the period of the 1720s; and he adds one pertinent, if scientifically inexact comment, that 'the stone being a kind of marble, or rather granite, is always moist and dewy in winter, which proves damp and unwholesome, and rots the furniture'. As Mr H. C. Brentnall (to whom I owe much of the information in this chapter) has pointed out, sarsen is not porous, but hard and impermeable, so hard that the damp condenses on its surface. Four rooms in the farmhouse under the cliff are paved with sarsen slabs, which are held to foretell the weather. When the barometer drops, and the air is filled with moisture, the floors look wringing wet, surprisingly wet, as if they had been newly washed.

Stukeley was an observer, not a builder, not a man who knew the vernacular traditions of building; and it seems to me that the waterproof nature of sarsen must have been well recognised. The walls of old houses, as everyone knows, frequently take up moisture from the ground, because they lack those damp courses which are now laid through them. Sarsen foundations and footings do in fact behave as a species of damp course: damp may condense on sarsen, but if the blocks are well chosen, if the ones pierced with ancient rootholes are rejected, the water cannot ascend. There is never much wrong with the chalk at the point where chalk and sarsen come together.

If Richard Symonds, Aubrey, Stukeley and the Borough accounts are the written evidence of the use of sarsens, the local churches show how much the sarsenry tradition goes back beyond the sixteenth century. In the walls of one thirteenth-century church between the cliff and the downs there are sarsens abundantly; some in the rough, and at the foot of the walls, some roughly squared, some blue or grey, some reddish brown, some of that kind of sarsen, little used in the later, best work, in which chunks of flint are embedded. They are an extraordinary mixture, these church walls, odd bits of limestones, flints, sarsens-with-flints, cut sarsens, raw sarsens – all in a kind of coloured rag-carpetwork of stone. In a neighbouring church, less ancient, in fact of the early fourteenth century, sarsen has been used with much more determination and purpose. Large, squared blocks rise from ground to eaves, though the quoins of the buildings are neatly made of a tough limestone. Now and then an even-faced block, with its original reddish rind and rootholes, has been inserted. The tall fifteenth-century tower of precise limestone is founded on huge rough sarsens, exactly in the manner of a nineteenth-century brick wall. Alongside this church a big range of thatched farm buildings and barns of the eighteenth or nineteenth century are for the most part made of sarsen, quoined with brick; and there is little difference between the two sets of walling separated by some 400 years. In the farmhouse district below the cliff, the one church of the fifteenth century rests two of its limestone buttresses full upon unhewn sarsens, one of them more than a foot thick, four feet long and nearly four feet wide.

Not counting the hardish limestone of the lower chalk for the minute, the line of the cliff and its farms lies in between two possible hard building rocks: these sarsen stones on the down and the rocks of the Corallian series, which exist beyond the clay. The rough Coral Rag is better for garden walls and retaining walls than for houses. The calcareous sand, stones and the sandy limestones associated with it are fit for building, and have been much used, as we shall see, particularly in the south-western area of the cliff. But these limestones and sandstones, though nearer at hand, had to be quarried. The sarsen lay on the surface; moreover, an easy gradient of five to six miles stretched from the sarsens to the farmsteads. In a space of some 250 or 300 years, huge quantities were brought down by waggon or sledge for house-building, and for many uses beside. In their bulk the sarsen boulders varied. There was one (which has been broken up) in the structure of Avebury which was estimated to weigh ninety tons. Larger boulders must have been roughly split up *in situ*, and the big pieces transported, to be subdivided again on the spot. Small boulders were brought down whole. As though they had fallen off sledge or waggon, or it had been found necessary to lighten the burden, one finds a good many small sarsens, or sarsen blocks, lying beside the tracks on the way down to the farms (just as one huge sarsen on the downs, evidently moved at one time, is thought to have been abandoned on its prehistoric transit to Avebury). Round the farm, and round every farmhouse, and round the village, one can see lumps of sarsen which, after all, were never used.

In the buildings the ratio of chalk to sarsen is different above and below the cliff. Below, I can think of no houses or farm buildings, and only a few walls, built wholly or mainly of sarsen. The bulk of the material is always chalk, which lay nearer, and could be quarried off the escarpment without much trouble, without having to sink pits, without having to remove an overlay of soil and poorer stone. Up above, the sarsen was still easier to procure. There, the chalk either had laboriously to be brought up from the cliff, or taken laboriously from pits sunk in the fields. Below the cliff, sarsen is the stuff for foundations and footings. Above the cliff, although much chalk was used, whole walls, whether of cowshed or waggon lodges, or cottages or churches, were built of sarsen from ground right up to roof. Now and then, some six feet of sarsen were laid, and then capped for the sake of neatness with accurately cut chalk – for about sixteen inches. But there are parishes eighty per cent sarsen, in everything from retaining walls to farms and church. This differing ratio, within a couple of miles, illustrates very well the older dependence of architecture upon local geology.

Generally, the earlier the building, the rougher the sarsen in its walls. By the nineteenth century, the sarsen was often neatly cut and squared into smallish blocks; but for foundations, the sarsen was left rough, whatever the date. There was little point in dressing it, since no more was required than a roughly level surface for the chalk or the brick to lie upon (though to make that easier, a single course of bricks was occasionally set first upon the sarsen before the chalk began). Such footings have a warm and comfortable appearance, from the original ruddiness of the stone. For later buildings of finer workmanship, and for retaining walls, the squared sarsen is built of courses of regular height, lessening in thickness towards the top. Even then, even when cut and squared, sarsen varies in colour. White to a whitish-grey, is predominant, but some blocks are shades of brown and pink. The sand grains sparkle in the sunlight, and their surface tones are modified by lichen – mainly by a close grey lichen. The orange and yellow lichens seem to find sarsen less agreeable than the lime mortar in between the blocks; so the curious effect occurs of grey or whitish sarsens picked out by mortar lines of orange and yellow. (With sarsen, by the way, a lime mortar should always be used. The stone is not absorbent enough for Portland cements.)

The retaining walls to gardens or cattle ponds are laid dry. A retaining wall to the Ashton farmhouse garden shows three courses above ground, surmounted by a privet hedge, the two lower courses of a ten-inch depth, the top course of nine. Most of the blocks are fifteen to sixteen inches long, though some are as much as three feet. Nearly all the boundary walls of brick have invisible foundations of sarsen. A four-foot brick wall in front of the farmhouse (capped with sandy limestone from the quarries below the Corallian rocks) has a sarsen foundation going down nearly as deep as the wall, a tough obstacle which exasperated the workmen when they had to burrow under the wall to bring in a water-pipe. One realises that if the sarsen workmanship is often crude to the eye, it was done thoroughly and effectively

Even if sarsen can be cleft and cut and shaped, it cannot be called a tractable stone. The bluish, shining sarsen is almost impossible to split; other sarsen blocks will cleave like slate along the grain, but even then I fancy sarsen would be useless to a sculptor, useless even to a monumental mason. Deep, clean lettering on the harder kinds of sarsen would hardly be feasible. So in building it gives itself more to effects of massiveness and colour than to effects of architectural delicacy. It has the rough virtues of looking simple and remaining more or less for ever. It does not disintegrate, it weathers hardly at all (as one can see in the fourteenth-century walls of the church). It can bear enormous weight. It has, in fact, been a farmer's utility stone – a stone for which he has found plenty of uses other than building. Small pieces make an excellent metal for paths, yards or doorways. The Ashton farmyard is concreted, but one or two yards around are cobbled with small knobs of sarsen. At Ashton Farm and on many of the farms a six-foot width of sarsen cobbles has been laid outside the cowsheds, to give the farmer and his men clean access. The doorways to farm buildings are usually cobbled with sarsens for some distance out. The horses clatter over sarsens into a sarsen-cobbled stable at Ashton, at the end of the large barn. It is an old stable, but the sarsen cobbles, battered by iron shoes for a hundred years or so, are scarcely worn (which is true of the paths of squared sarsens which lead into most of the local churchyards). Sarsen monoliths were used for making gateposts, but mostly above the cliff, on ground without an abundance of timber. Below, there was wood available, and it was not worth squandering a block of sarsen, which had to be carried several miles. For drains in gateways and under lanes and roads, the stone came in handy, though for this use its durability has sometimes been undone by its weight. For years a by-road in the village below Ashton has been waterlogged, rutted and almost impassable in winter, because the drain carrying the stream under the roadway was blocked. This drain was one of the first subjects which the Parish Meeting discussed when it was convened again after the Second World War. Action was pressed upon the County Council. Its men came, and opened up the road and the drain, to find that it was made of three huge pieces of sarsen each of a ton weight or so, carrying the road, and resting on either side on smaller, but still large sarsen blocks. The weight had sunk the drain more than a foot, and the sarsens had to be lifted and removed by block and tackle, before they could be replaced by two earthenware pipes. Another minor use I have noticed is laying sarsen for a footstone between the wooden uprights of a wicket-stile, or squeeze-belly.

Down here along the cliff no work in sarsen – in newly fetched sarsen – has been carried out within living memory. No one recalls anything of the simple problems of splitting and dressing it, though the stone is still recognised and named by everyone. But within ten miles, in the downland parishes, sarsen was being cut, carted and used in the twenties and thirties. The author of the Geological Survey's memoir on the district noticed the sarsen footing 'of a new barn or waggon lodge' on the downs in 1923. Mr H. C. Brentnall, in his excellent pamphlet on sarsens, written in 1930, says that 'those who have watched this district for the last twenty or thirty years have seen the wolf at work in many a fold of the grey wethers, daily devouring apace and nothing said'. He describes how the sarsens have all gone from a wood where they lay among the bluebells under the oaks and birches, have all been broken up for the road-metal of a neighbouring town (in the past, sarsens have been much used for making roads), how there was a demand in the twenties for sarsen kerbs and setts, and how after work with wedges and sledgehammer 'at last the almost dazzling cubes are lying in even rows on the down beside a snowy heap of dust and fragments'. A Geological Survey memoir of 1858 talks both of their use in road-making and of sarsens being 'broken by the hammer into rectangular blocks for paving stone', which the farmhouse flooring shows to have been an old practice. The chapel of Marlborough College is built in part of sarsen stones. Sarsen has been exported. It has been used, and is still used, in repairs on Windsor Castle (though sarsen occurred nearer to Windsor); there are local railway viaducts of sarsen. But sentiment seems to have turned against the despoiling of these ancient geological remnants (which are more widely scattered round the south than one realises). Some are preserved under the National Trust; more would be cared for, no doubt, under the new scheme for Geological Reserves.

Scenically it would indeed be a shame to lose them from the downs; and that even so many survive is due perhaps to the arresting of construction and development on farms which came some sixty years ago with the great depression in agriculture. Yet, looking back, it is clear one can carry sentiment too far. The stones were there, after all, in an area of chalk, and the stones were used – and paid, and still pay, a good dividend in the solidity of buildings and the easing of the filth and the tasks of farming. The district would have been in a poor way without sarsens; for without this mating of the hard and the less hard, the use of the blocky chalk could never have been so general nor could it ever have lasted for so long.

*Chalk, with brick quoin, in the waggon-lodge, split and weathered,
owing to the decay of the thatch.*

CHALK

CHALK DOMINATES the farms, stretching along above them with an illimitable supply. The height of the escarpment above the farm chimneys is about a hundred feet, but the beds of this thickness of the Lower Chalk vary in durability, hardness and solidity; and one realises straight away how chalk more than most stones has to be 'learnt'. It is a stone much inferior to sarsen, in sheer stoniness, even if it is more tractable and does not condense moisture upon its surface. Sarsen could be cut and used straight away. One needed an eye to distinguish between good and bad sarsen, between clear, clean-grained boulders and boulders with flints, or boulders pierced too deep by the holes left in the sarsen in the days when it was uncompacted sand and the roots of conifers pierced down through it. One needed to learn its nature under tools and to learn such methods of splitting the big stones by fire and water as William Stukeley described. But the inferior chalk demanded more; it demanded a more elaborate traditional technique – which bed to quarry, cutting, weathering, protection in the wall itself. It was a technique which must have taken generations in the learning. Knowledge of it has now died away: no local record of the technique exists in print, for chalk was a commonplace substance beside the mysterious, intruding sarsen stones, and it is difficult now to find out the details. Exposed, unprotected chalk weathers very quickly, quarries quickly tumble in, are covered up and disappear.

In the tougher building-stone districts a few miles away one can often track down the site of ancient mediaeval quarries, long ago filled up, by the survival in field names of the Middle English 'quarre'; but there seem to be no such names to point to old chalk workings. So far as one can tell from the indications, and the remnants of memory, the bed which was hewn and crowbarred out lay about twenty-two feet down from the more or less level crest of the escarpment. The plain above dips slightly in a shallow bowl before it begins to rise again towards the downs, so quarrymen round the upper villages and farms would have found this hard bed of building chalk anything from five to ten feet under the fields; and there are people who still faintly recollect the sinking of such pits.

The building band was between six and ten feet wide, was hard and grey when exposed. The chalk was 'broken out' or 'fallen out' of the quarry, that is to say, it was pitched out in big boulders which broke with the fall. It was then sawn to odd sizes, 'random sizes', as required; and the blocks were stacked with air spaces in between, and with a covering of straw. In other parts of England where the Lower Chalk was used, it was weathered in large masses, which revealed 'irregular joints and bedding planes that are invisible in the freshly exposed stone'. Mr Clough Williams-Ellis has written of chalk quarrying that the longer blocks 'are kept to dry before building in the better, and the sun and wind of at least a year' (under protection from the rain) 'should be allowed to play upon them to dry out their natural sap and keep them "frost-proof"'.

Uncertain signs of quarrying exist all along the escarpment, beside the roads or tracks rising up to the plain; but if it is not easy to tell how old the workings are, how far back precisely the local tradition of using the chalk extends, one thing is clear: as with sarsens, chalk was certainly used by the mediaeval church builders in the neighbourhood, as it was used elsewhere in England. In the church, whose walls contain flints, cream-coloured limestone and sarsen, there is one piece of interior walling in chalk, small chalk blocks carefully cut and fitted. In another church, a sixteenth-century gentleman in armour and his wife, carved out of chalk which could have been raised within a hundred yards, kneel facing each other in two niches.

The quality of this local chalk probably compares ill with chalk quarried from the same formation in other counties. Totternhoe Stone from Bedfordshire, the similar stone from Burwell in Cambridgeshire, Beer Stone from Devonshire – all come from the Lower Chalk, and have all been worked from early times for churches and for secular buildings. Beer Stone, for example, was brought up from Devon for St Stephen's crypt in the Houses of Parliament (see *The Stones of London*, by J. V. Elsden and J. A. Howe, who also say that much chalk was used in the outer walls of the Tower of London and in Windsor Castle). Churches apart, the oldest piece of chalk work that I know along the cliff is the huge fireplace at Ashton Farm, spanned by an oak beam more than seven feet long. On either side, giving support to the beam, pieces of chalk have been built in, two feet two inches high, four feet deep and ten inches wide. The inner edge of each block has been chamfered, the chamfering ending above the hearth in crude ornamentation. Another more finely wrought fireplace exists on the floor up above. It was painted over, cleverly grained in shades of dark green, some time in the last fifty years. The carving was clean and sharp under the paint, and the material was thought to be a more cohesive freestone, until a child knocked a piece out with a hammer. The two certain things are that chalk was extensively employed here in the sixteenth century, inside and out, continuing in general use until about 1850 or 1860, in occasional, dwindling use until some time later; and that enough of it was used in the Middle Ages for the properties of chalk to be well understood later on, in the great building period of the 1570s and 1580s.

Once again, in the farm buildings there were three ways of employing chalk, according to differences of date and skill. It was built up in Cyclopean, irregular courses, very roughly shaped and faced; or it was also meticulously cut into large blocks, usually, for the main courses, showing a face of fourteen by sixteen inches, the courses decreasing in depth towards the eaves – in other words, a rough and less rough ashlar construction. The third way – typical certainly of later, and the best, chalk building round about 1800 – was to cut the chalk into 'bricks' varying much in length from ten inches and in depth from six inches to two and a half. The absence of uniformity through the district, the differences in one village, in one set of farm buildings, in one house, in the ways in which the chalk no less than the sarsen is used, suggest that much of the building – the stonework at least – was carried out by the farmers and their men and by the cottagers, though chalk chimneys show finer workmanship: the stones were fitted close and tight against danger of fire. Woodwork throughout the houses and the barns, in the timbering of the roofs, and in the farms in such older gates and gateposts of oak as still exist, follows more of a pattern, depending as it did upon a more intricate skill, upon professionalism. The roughest chalk building is in the cottages (built by the cottagers themselves) and in some of the farm buildings. Farmhouses of chalk, and farm buildings generally, have sarsen foundations and quoins of brick or sarsen: the cottages are often chalk throughout. Their old earth floors have disappeared, but they are damper round the base of the walls than the larger houses built on the waterproof sarsen.

The general method of construction was to raise two thicknesses of chalk block and fill in the centre with chippings and rubble. The walls are thick, up to two feet and more, and care and tenderness for the nature of the chalk were shown in the way the houses fit to the points of the compass. If the chalk gets waterlogged, and is then attacked by frost, it flakes away in curved fragments. One soon finds it is the chalk walls which face south-west, into the prevailing rainy quarter, which have been damaged most by weathering. Many houses are placed, so to speak, square to the compass – Ashton farmhouse is one – so that they present only a corner, not a full-faced wall, to the south-westerly winds. A chalk wall which does look to the south-west not infrequently has a face of bricks; and the chimneys above tile or thatch level are usually brick, not chalk, except on the poorer houses. One cannot protect a chimney; in fact, on the cottages one can often see chalk chimneys almost eaten away in the middle, tapering in like a wasp waist. Deflect a chalk wall slightly from the south-west to south, or west, and at once the difference in weathering is visible. On the north or east side of a chalk house, the blocks have seldom exfoliated at all. On the north side of Ashton farmhouse, someone, perhaps a son of the RS

Chalk, rashly used instead of sarsen, under a garden wall of brick.

who built or rebuilt the house in 1668, has cut his initials 'MS' together
with the date '1714' in a block, and the lettering remains as defined and
clear as ever. On other houses initials and dates carved fifty years earlier
are still in good condition.

Chalk is not treacherous: it simply needs common sense and protection
– protection by placing of the house and by the projection of the eaves.
Newcomers to the district often try making rockeries of chalk blocks, to
find them all split into fragments by the end of February; and they are
not alone in being deceived. As knowledge of chalk building has declined,
and as thatch has decayed, farm buildings, houses and cottages have been
given new roofs of slate or galvanised, sometimes scarcely projecting at
all, sometimes without gutters; and the chalk has weathered away more in
five years than in the previous fifty. Thatched eaves should come out the
best part of two feet from the walls, should carry the rain clear and should
thus keep the soil near the footings dry. From a properly roofed building of
chalk one should be able to enjoy that pleasant sight recorded by the poet
Bampfylde in one of his sonnets – that pleasant sight and sound of a line
of pendulous drops from the roof:

> Silent the swallow sits beneath the thatch
> And vacant hind hangs pensive o'er his hatch,
> Counting the frequent drops from reeded eaves.

Now and then in the neighbourhood one finds a wall made of chalk
with its own thatched roof, projecting twenty or twenty-two inches on
either side. Two genteel houses built of chalk, one late in the eighteenth-
century, one round about 1830, show how well this need of protection was
understood. Both are roofed with slates, but the eaves come out as far and
farther than thatch. The latest building in the village which is chiefly made
of chalk, and which can be dated with certainty, is the church, erected in
1846 and 1847. It has, or had, a roof of stone tiles, and its chalk walls were
completely faced with a good hard freestone.

Properly used, there is no doubt that chalk is weatherproof and valuable.
Yet one must say that many chalk walls are now in bad condition, not

because of the material, not through the ignorance of later generations, but because of the builders. Either the chalk was not weathered long enough for it to show its planes of weakness, or it was not placed on its quarry bed: it has split vertically, and weathered, and started falling to bits. Patching it up with cement is no great help, since cement and chalk are not too inclined to marry. But do not doubt the toughness of chalk. It may crack under a hammer or a knock; yet try making a hole in a chalk wall with a Rawlplug drill, or try driving a nail into chalk, or cutting through eighteen inches of chalk wall to insert the draining pipe for a bath or lavatory. It leads to blasphemy and a tired arm, and, by comparison, piercing a block of oolitic limestone is mere simplicity.

Elsewhere than in this district the oldest English building in chalk dates back, I believe, some 800 years, and in our own time chalk has been employed, and well employed, by the late Sir Edwin Lutyens. Mr Clough Williams-Ellis, who has advocated its re-introduction, has summed up the case for chalk by saying that 'it improves mightily with keeping . . . for years after being built into the walls of a house chalk will continue to dry and harden . . . it will quickly revenge itself on those neglecting its just demands for a sound roof and a proper damp course.'

A chalk, chalk and brick, chalk and sarsen house has its own particular beauty. In some farmhouses most of the sarsen is invisible; the level of the flowerbeds has risen gradually, and the point of having the sarsen foundation has been forgotten. Ashton farmhouse sits firmly upon blocks which rise behind snowdrops and lilies of the valley, and seems to have an unshiftable, everlasting solidity. The roof, partly of stone tiles, mainly of thatch, the walls, with large areas of chalk against large areas of brick, sometimes intermixed – all the different substances blend very well. The colour of the chalk in the walls varies according to the weather, as the geologist of the local *Memoir* remarked: 'The aspect of the stone depends on the amount of moisture present. Of mellow, sunny appearance in dry weather, it quickly assumes a dull, brownish-grey tint at the onset of rain.' Yet that dull brownish-grey is not unpleasant, and wet or damp, a chalk wall never has a uniformity of tone. Though it has not the variation of colour of a sarsen wall (the tidiness of chalk in good condition is preferable, I think), the chalk itself will vary from white to a pinkish white, or yellowish white, and grey. Some blocks are stained with rust from pockets of decomposed iron pyrites, some have the round markings of a grey lichen. The old lime mortar outlines the blocks with smooth bands of cleaner white (though sometimes a palish brown mortar was used). Beneath thatch, grey and brown and heavily tufted and cushioned with moss, or beneath the warmth and irregularity of stone tiles, and above the ruddiness of sarsen, or interspersed with the red and lichen-yellow of brick quoins, chalk left with its own natural face has homeliness and propriety: it has a cleanliness which is neither smartly trim nor dull. On some of the later buildings, in which the chalk has been very carefully smoothed and cut, the appearance is a bit too trim. On earlier or rougher buildings, the chalk has no mathematically accurate surface, tool marks are visible, and the light upon the walls is broken up by shadow. Moreover, large patches of chalk in the cliff behind are exposed by landslides, so that there is, here, a certain positive congruity between architecture and landscape.

In modern times, local owners of chalk houses have been afraid to let the chalk alone. Ashton farmhouse is one of the lucky exceptions. Its chalk is chalk and visible as such. But chalk, through taking its revenge, in Mr Williams-Ellis's phrase, upon ignorance and neglect, has acquired a bad name. Builders now are scared of it, owners are scared, and have it concealed under an often unnecessary 'protection' of whitewash, or colour wash, or a uniformly puritan skin of grey cement. The cement-wash flakes off, diversifying dullness with an ugly patchwork of grey and white; incidentally, the washes hide (which is a pity) the dates and names carved on the chalk in earlier centuries, which demonstrate how well it can stand up to the weather. I fancy this concealment was never practised when the building nature of the chalk was better realised. Mr Williams-Ellis recommends treating the surface with a silicate, or drying fluid, which would act like fixative on a watercolour, protect the chalk and do nothing to injure, smudge or hide its delicate tones.

Undoubtedly many chalk buildings will disappear within the next twenty years. The thatch grows thin, water comes through, the timbers rot, the chalk is soaked, a patch of the outer facing of chalk comes off and the damp and frost pierce inwards to the rubble. Before one can turn round, the cottage or farm building is nine-tenths on the ground. Rather than patch and repair beyond a certain point, the farmer will allow destruction to become complete. If it is one of his own buildings, he will either not replace it at all, or replace it with an efficient, styleless building of composition blocks and asbestos tiles. One tenant farmer under the cliff, talking to me of repairs and the concreting of his farmyard, remarked that land tax took away some half of the rent, and the other half, in one year, had gone on the concreting. Certainly few of the old farm buildings of chalk are adapted, and few of the yards are laid out, for a modern mechanised agriculture, for the size and behaviour of modern implements, or for the clean production of milk. One is back at the tilted nature of farm life, which is over on its side, instead of rocking sensitively to and fro like a logan stone.

The nature of the chalk means that one must use it where it lies inert, where it performs its function simply by sitting still, under cover, block upon block. It is true that farmers sometimes use it, broken up small, to mix with cement into concrete; and if enough cement has been added, this chalk concrete does last well enough even under farmyard traffic; but, beyond walling, and now and again monumental sculpture inside churches and ornamental fireplaces, I can think of no other building use to which it has been put. Even the two chalk statues I am thinking of have lost their noses.

There is indeed a kind of chalk walling I have not mentioned. Wells round about are carefully lined with blocks of chalk, cut and squared: and down a well, away from frost and variations of temperature, the chalk sits still in the best of conditions. The capstone of these wells is now and then a slab of sarsen pierced by a circular hole.

Early-nineteenth-century bricks, dark and from the downland kilns.

THE BRICKS AND THE BRICK KILNS

IF YOU LOOK at a country church of the Middle Ages – for instance, the thirteenth-century church of this district above and under the cliff – the one thing you are not likely to find in its walls is brick, unless the church is in Norfolk or Suffolk. Brick there may be inserted in late additions and in restoration work, but it is a commonplace to observe that generally it comes late into English architecture, even if it is one of the ancient building materials of the world. In the rubble wall – the south wall – of that particular church, there is everything except brick, everything that the builders could scrape together locally and that promised durability against the weather. Bricks came in, by way of East Anglia, in the Middle Ages; but they were costly, they spread slowly, and were little used in vernacular building in the homes of ordinary men of ordinary means until, so it appears, the seventeenth and the eighteenth centuries. Thus the small square block of stone on which Mr 'RS' of Ashton Farm has had his initials carved, and the year 1668, is let into a square chimney-top cap of dark-red bricks which rise above the lines of chalk. Brick proved handy and neat for the quoins and the gables of the chalk houses, a reversal of the ordinary practice of building with brick and adding the quoins in stone; but it must signify the expense and difficulty of obtaining bricks down here in the south that their early employment was in the chimneys alone, in that exposed portion of the building for which chalk had proved unsuitable. The brick quoins come later. The earlier farmhouses, the earlier portions of the houses refashioned in the seventeenth century, are all finished off at the quoins with large chalk blocks, and in such buildings the chalk is carried up through the gables to the thatch. Even when brick does come to be generally built into the crude vernacular of this district, it is used without fancy. The chimneys all rise rectangular and plain, and high so that the thatch is cleared by any sparks. The quoins, in the better work, are carefully and neatly bonded into the chalk; but in brick walls hereabouts it is no good looking for anything fanciful or decorative, anything which has found its way into the large expensive quartos of English county architecture, anything except good, plain brickwork, in English bond.

Sooner or later, bricks were made in the neighbourhood; a manufacture, like the quarrying of chalk, which has now disappeared. Coming late, when placenames were well established, and disappearing within two centuries, the brickyards like the chalk quarries again have left no names behind, and the clay-pits which fed them have for the most part either filled up to shallow troughs or changed into ponds. But the kilns are marked, and were then in action, on the Ordnance Map of 1828. A few were out on the clay below the farms, four miles or so from the cliff, and were used within memory. One building in the nearest small town – a brewery – was built from bricks whose clay had been dug out in the brewery foundations. But those which produced the best bricks, red and crimson and vitrified to a dark green, existed where one would least expect to find them – up on the sarsen-stone country, up on the downs, in a lonely area, exposed and cold. These kilns, seven of them in 1828, if the map is to be relied upon, still standing in 1858, lay on either side of a long 'green road', which goes with a wide view of the world past tumuli and sarsens and sarsen burial chambers. One can picture them – picture the contrast of business and loneliness, smoke and debris and flocks of sheep and clumps of naked elder, as the whole might have been drawn by some such artist as de Loutherbourg, Wright of Derby or James Ward. 'Pit-coal', as it was then called to distinguish it from charcoal, was used by the end of the eighteenth century in the downland villages and farms (I have a record of coal costing one and threepence a hundredweight to the cottager hereabouts, in 1858, so one may fancy the kiln waggons going out red with brick and dragging back up the slope of the downs black with coal).

Some of the kilns one can still trace by fragments of coal among the elders, fragments of brick, clinker and vitrified flint. A particular kiln, or the site of a particular kiln, is marked by a slight hollow alongside the green road, which has filled up with nettles. Poke up among the nettles, and one can find broken, discarded bricks, well burnt and hard, some red, some burnt much darker, and some vitrified on the surface. Thirty yards away is a clay-pit, red under the elder trees, half filled up by the slide of earth, and with kettles and pans and bits of bedstead from a nearby, and now deserted, farm in a side valley of the downs. A hollow track, with a big elder blocking it as it rises from the pit, is still just visible, pointing towards the kiln. This brick-clay, so unexpected on the chalk, is part of a superficial deposit of 'clay-with-flints'. There are loams of three different colours, according to the geological memoir: this reddish loam, a buff and a light brown, here and there clean enough for burning into bricks. But evidently, with little water up on the downs, the maker and his men took no great trouble to render the clay much cleaner than it was. The fragments of brick are full of largish chunks of flint, which nevertheless is useful, since it makes it easy around the farms to distinguish downland bricks from the bricks manufactured on the plain out of a brick-earth, which contains, not flint, but impurities of a different stone. Knowledge and working of these clay-pits may have gone back long before the nineteenth, eighteenth or seventeenth centuries. There are early cultivation terraces on the downs within a couple of miles one way, where one can pick up sherds of a buff pottery. Buff and a darker burnt pottery of the Iron Age crops up within a camp nearby; and two and a half miles the other way, below the downs, quantities of Neolithic pottery have been excavated on a now classic site – dark pottery of a gritty ware such as might, one supposes, have been made from these gritty, flinty loams. So it is at least conceivable that, from the earliest manufacture of pottery in Neolithic England, these beds have been exploited by potters through the Iron Age, the Roman and the Saxon eras and the Middle Ages, down to the establishment of these now forgotten brick kilns of the last three centuries.

There is a chapelry elsewhere in the county named Crockerton, on which John le Crocker was living in 1268, and Stephen le Crocker twenty years later. At the nearby Potter's Hill, Richard le Poter lived in 1252. Crockery was being made there in the seventeenth century, and bricks and tiles are still being made there from the deposits used by the 'crockers' and 'potters' of the thirteenth century. Such a continuity, incapable as it may be of proof, would be no more surprising than the continuance of a farm or a village on the site of a Saxon 'tun', or the fact that the Saxon-named Cotmarsh, below the cliff, 'marsh marked by cottages', answers very nearly to its name and is still a huddle of cottages surrounded by waterlogged fields.

Just as more sarsen is used in farms and villages nearer to the supply above the cliff, and less sarsen below the cliff, so more of these dark-red, greenish-black, vitrified bricks are visible in the buildings the nearer they are to the kilns. On Ashton and in Netton most of the bricks came from the plain. In the upper villages, every bit of walling which is not sarsen or chalk is made of downland brick, often red and dark-green used together in patterns.

One can tell something of the age of the bricks used in the brick portions of the house and the farm buildings and the neighbouring farms by their size. They vary in length from nine to nine and a half inches, but are all two-and-a-half-inch bricks – two and a half inches deep, as against the three-inch depth of the modern and later nineteenth-century bricks. All the brick fragments around the kiln have this two-and-a-half-inch measurement. One local peculiarity, in many walls such as the long south wall to the farmhouse garden at Ashton Farm, and in the walls of not a few farm buildings, is the use of what appears to be a brick of unusual depth – four inches. In fact, these are thin hollow walls in which the bricks are laid on their sides, instead of flat, and are keyed across the hollow by 'enders'. No doubt the reason was economy, bricks being wider than they are deep – jerry building in other words. Yet these thin walls on their sarsen foundations remain strong; and the unfamiliarity of effect is light and pleasing.

There is no doubting the hardness, the good burning of the old bricks, whether from above the cliff or below. Some of them, from fallen calf-stalls, were used for a garden path and steps; but the last step had to be finished off with modern machine-made bricks more regular in shape, though less compact, less weighty. Within four years these modern bricks have been skinned off by the frost, skinned off into powder. The old bricks, made no doubt before 1850, are still solid and stony as ever.

THE HARDER BUILDING STONES

HERE were two available sources of harder limestones. I have mentioned one, the quarries under the Corallian. From the best of these Ashton Farm and the village are six miles away. The other source is some eight miles off, where there exist quarries which produced (and, wonderful to say, still produce) excellent limestone of Portland and Purbeck types. (Round these Portland and Purbeck quarries, by the way, there has grown up since the 1830s a squalid industrial town built, as though there was no stone within a hundred miles, almost entirely of brick.) From one set of quarries or the other, very little stone has ever been employed in the Ashton buildings, or round about. In the farmhouse itself such stone occurs only once – in the block let into the chimney bearing the founder's initials and the date. This carved stone is the only scrap of fanciful ornament in the actual substance of the house: lettering, border and layout are good and at odds rather with the seemly crudeness and comfort of the building.

By a few miles, again, these harder limestones lay too far off for 'economic' use. Yet it is instructive to see how much of the stone was carted, difficulty or no difficulty, expense or no expense, to be built into the churches. The church towers are made entirely of good limestone, above sarsen foundations. But churches were always a special case: money was spent on them, faith modified meanness; difficulties, up to a point, were disregarded in the interests of faith. A church had to be durable like eternity, so stone was used when most houses around were still made of timber and wattle-and-daub. One cause, in fact, of the sixteenth-century change from timber construction to stone in many parts of England was the dissolution of the monasteries. Fine eternal buildings, aggregations of stone ready quarried and shaped, were sold – sold cheap, demolished, carted off. For contrast, compare the faith which made Norman church and cathedral builders bring over Caen stone, that limestone from Normandy of which Canterbury Cathedral is built. And in much the same way it was faith, rising above difficulties and expense, which made the builders of Stonehenge disregard difficulties and distance, and transport the tall 'blue stones' of dolerite from the Prescelly Hills in Pembrokeshire, nearly 150 miles away; and more, by the probable route of the transporters. What one will do for faith, one will not do always for other men, for one's descendants, or even for one's own comfort or benefit; and as C. F. Innocent says in his *Development of English Building Construction* (a book necessary to everyone concerned with the vernacular architecture of his own district), 'greater cheapness . . . has ever been one of the motive forces' in the way English building has developed. It is disconcerting – disconcerting to one's notion that this motive of cheap and cheaper still, which activates us in the twentieth century, did not activate our more virtuous ancestors. The poet William Barnes complained of nineteenth-century architecture that 'we have churches of a fine, high-wrought street end, and brick walls behind, out of man's sight (poor Pugin's eyesore!), as if the builders worked not for good, but for man'; and Barnes quoted:

> They build the front, upon my word
> As fine as any abbey;
> But thinking they might cheat the Lord
> They made the back part shabby.

The faith behind nineteenth-century church building was like the faith behind *Hymns A and M* – it was what Coventry Patmore, when he contrasted those with the religious poetry of the seventeenth century, called a fire-mist instead of a flame. But alas, as we know, even flame in the days of flame burnt with intermissions. If stone was indeed used in

A thatched barn with sarsen at the bottom corner of the brickwork to prevent damage by farm vehicles. Galvanised iron pushed under the thatch.

country churches when men used timber and wattle for themselves, there is evidence enough in church and cathedral construction of the past, as well as in the more recent farmhouses, to show that our own ruthless inclination to cheapness, though more developed, is not original. And how quickly one discovers that fact, the moment one begins to pierce beneath the match-boarding and wallpaper of an old farmhouse, the moment one begins to uncover the amount of elm used where oak ought to have been used, the amount of sapwood, now soft and rotten, employed instead of hard, seasoned, durable timbers! Still, there is a difference between 'greater cheapness' as 'one of the motive forces', and greater cheapness as, simply, the motive force.

The style and seemliness remained. The builder knew too little about stresses and strains to risk cutting his timbers down near to the point of

The waggon-lodge. Chalk, brick, elm-boards and thatch.

danger; and so the Ashton farmhouse of 1668 will still outlast the council houses of 1920 or the newer council houses of 1946 which are its not-so-distant neighbours. 'Greater cheapness' and 'jerry-building' in the seventeenth century often meant that portions of a house would last only two and a half centuries instead of five centuries or six.

Coming back to stone, the south-eastern end of the cliff is only two miles from some of those ancient quarries; so thereabouts, despite sarsen and brick, despite the chalk, still cheaper, still nearer at hand and available perhaps on the farmer's own holding, the proportion of hard limestone to chalk, and so on, in the buildings is much higher. One farmhouse close up under the cliff, in a site, even for these cliff sites, unusually high and commanding, is made entirely, so far as one can see, of this harder stone, and not of the chalk which rises fifty yards behind. It is an early-nineteenth-century house. Yet here again the nearby cottages are chalk, and are now in a bad way. A farmhouse immediately across the lane is chalk; and so is, or was, the earlier farmhouse ('Bubbe's Tun') within four fields' distance.

Travel the six miles home again to Ashton Farm and at any rate one shed with a loft over it shows a face of this same hard stone – or to be exact two walls of it are so built, the south-west wall against the weather, and the east wall. The rest of it, away from the weather, is once more the customary chalk. Even above the hard stone in the two walls, as though not enough had been carted for the job, chalk, finely cut, has been laid for the last few courses under the thatch. And, as I have said, the church of 1846–7 is faced with good-quality stone over chalk. Coral Rag, which occurs not only six miles off, but within a mile or two, has been brought over and employed, not only for the late rockeries and the border edges, but for a few rough division walls in the cowyards. But it is a pitted, irregular, awkward stone, so there is little enough of it to be found. The Portland quarries, eight miles to the north-west, provided Ashton and the other farmsteads with stone, though not very much, for one purpose at least – capping the garden walls of brick upon sarsen. Flat slabs lie along the south wall of the kitchen garden. Slabs, well cut and bevelled, also cap the walls, at a more ceremonial, visible point – the walls along by the front door, bordering the front flower garden of jasmine, rose bush, syringa, soapwort and everlasting pea.

Where these front walls make a right-angled turn, the capstones do not just join, squarely, stone to stone, at the corner. The corner, the angle, is covered with a special right-angled piece, of good craftsmanship. The pity of it is that these garden walls, delicately crusted with rue-fern or rusty ceterach (both lime-loving species which root in the mortar between the bricks), or patched with the lemon-yellow of the garden fumitory, which is one of the favourite plants around here in farm and cottage gardens, are seldom repaired nowadays by the owner-occupiers. A section falls out, and the bricks are left lying where they fell. A capstone falls and breaks, and is never replaced. Or if the wall is repaired, a rough job is made with concrete, which is filled in to the height of the capstones on either side.

Local patriotism will not allow me to deny that the few old walls of oolitic or sandy limestone have a delicate surface pleasanter to the eye than the surfaces of chalk or sarsen. I pass the stone shed, or rather the shed partly of stone, daily on my way to the post office, and daily admire the speckling of light and shade on the walls, and the faint yellow of the lichen which grows over the whole of their extent. Yet there is much in favour of the variety which comes to the eye, the variety of sarsen, chalk and brick, and this occasional limestone. In the Cotswold villages away across the plain, however much they may be admired, however delicately the universal stone has weathered, the very universality is monotonous, is somewhat boring, and made more boring still by the fact that the one plant which now seems to be in universal favour throughout the Cotswold villages is the vulgarity of Aubrietia (a plant, I often think, which might well have been licensed to stay in its home in Southern Europe). The Cotswolds are aware of themselves, they say 'here we are to be admired'; and Aubrietia is the sign of self-consciousness. It is good to live in a district unsentimentalised, ill-equipped with inns, and unaware of its own existence – even in decay.

Talking of alien stones, there is one use and importation of them here (though not for building), which I am unable to explain. Why, in the past (they are more frequent over the cliff than below), did men go to the trouble of importing the enormous thin flags of limestone which are set up on end as stiles? There are many of these stone stiles, in one piece, four feet or so out of the ground and five feet long (below the cliff the wooden squeeze-bellies are more common). Why slabs of this kind, so difficult and expensive to drag from miles away, for such a humdrum employment? I fancy some of the same stone has often been laid to bridge over field drains for the passage of carts and waggons. But why not use sarsen? Why not stiles of two or three blocks of sarsen laid one on top of each other?

For walling around the farms one other material was used now and then, chalk 'dob'; but it is certainly uncommon now around and along the cliff. It was made of the local chalky mud mixed with chopped straw

– and maybe it was generally employed in the neighbourhood before the exploitation of the chalk and the sarsen began. Perhaps it was a relic of the distant past, like the continuing thatch upon houses and barns. One can see an analogy in Devon and Cornwall. Both those counties have plenty of excellent building stones. But it was only long after these stones were quarried for churches or castles – centuries afterwards, in fact – that they came into use (easy as they are to cleave and dress) for farmhouses, farm buildings and cottages. 'Cob' – the western equivalent of chalk dob – was preferred; and was employed, at least for cottages, even within the last hundred years. Slate also was not lacking in Cornwall, but thatch long persisted, in spite of Cornish slate, and its fine quality. One thinks of the 'groated' slate roofs – that is to say, slate roofs greyed over with cement, as an ancient original element of such a fishing town as Polperro;[*] but Jonathan Couch, who died in 1870, had known these houses covered, all of them, with thatch. Cost married the conservatism of tradition in these matters of cob and stone, and thatch and slate. Here, along the cliff, while the thatch has remained, the dob, if it was common, has almost disappeared. There is no dwelling house certainly, and I think no boundary wall or set of walls in a farm building within these few miles, which is made of dob; though I know of an old cowshed where it has been used (and where it remains) to finish off a chalk wall between the chalk and the thatch.

If there was a local tradition of using it, then the tradition, for some reason or other, weakened sooner than the cob tradition in, for example, East Cornwall, where, even now, cob buildings remain two a penny. Still, it is no great loss. Chalk dob, whitey-grey, lacks that warmness of tone, of pale browns and fawns, or in some parts of pale red, by which West Country cob-walling is made so pleasant.

[*] This practice, common also in Wales, may be a survival of the early habit of whitewashing or liming the thatch (cf. Innocent's *Development of English Building Construction*).

Moss-encrusted thatch on a cottage.

THATCH AND TILE

I is difficult nowadays to tell how good the local skill in thatching has been. Thatch was no doubt universal on the chalk buildings of the sixteenth century, the use of stone tiles coming in during the seventeenth and eighteenth centuries; and a great area of thatch still survives and makes a problem. Only three thatchers are now at work along the cliff, and one of them is more rick-thatcher in his skill than house-thatcher. The thatch one sees has been coarsely laid and finished, without, for instance, that Devonshire and Dorset translation of straw almost into another material, almost into a thick cloth, which curves and twists compactly and intimately around the windows, making, as William Barnes said, eyebrows above the eyes. And the problem is one of material as well as of labour. In good thatching areas, some corn is still specially grown for thatch, and specially reaped. Here the straw employed has all been through the threshing machine, is bruised and broken, and thereafter none too carefully selected. It is sad to see so much of the thatch in decay, with the spars sticking out till the roof looks like a shabby hedgehog, not only on cottages and farmhouses, but on the great wooden barns; and sad in no spirit of sentimentality for thatch, delightful as it looks in good shape; but because roof and building are allowed to go down together. I have seen four well-built, still useful barns fall to the ground in the last ten years because the thatch was neither renewed nor replaced; and other barns, from which the thatch has been stripped and replaced with galvanised iron, are going the same way. A sheet has been blown out of position, the timbers are exposed, another sheet blows aside. Nothing is done, and, at last, part of the timber framework rots and collapses. The roof above Ashton Farm is covered partly with stone tile and partly with thatch; its top thatch is twelve years old (it covers most of the seventeenth-century chalk portion and the nineteenth-century addition in brick) and it is now full of rain gullies and hollow patches, though it leaks only a little in the very heaviest rain. The big barn is thatched, and also needs, not repairing and patching, but re-covering. On another farm, as I mentioned in the first chapter, the main portion of the thatched barn fell long ago (not that it was not useful or used); most of the stable end still standing last year, still in use, left only a small, diminishing dry area for the horses and the harness, and the prize-winning cards of old agricultural shows tacked to the wall.

The Ashton barn was nearly burnt to the ground through carelessness a few years ago. The cowshed runs at right angles to the barn; and a milking machine, with its engine, was installed. The engine exhaust pipe they carried up just below the thatch; and for a year or so all went well. Living alongside, one could tell the time of day by the sudden steady throbbing of the engine at morning and afternoon milking. Then a spark from the exhaust set alight one corner of the vast flank of thatch. Only a quick phone call, hurried work with buckets and ladders, and the arrival of a fire engine saved a fire which would have destroyed the barn, several unthreshed ricks and the winter's hay. One would no longer have enjoyed the sight of the brown slope steaming away after a night's frost, as the sun rose on to it from behind the cliff, the sight of the tufts of moss wet and glimmering in the thaw. Thatch thoroughly in decay grows a strange intermingled crop. In summer the remaining thatch on the stable I have just spoken of was yellow with ragwort and deep pink with rosebay willowherb. Thatch which is still serviceable grows a crust of lichens as well as that most beautiful of all mosses, *Tortula ruralis* – the moss grows in smooth, rounded clumps. When the weather is dry, the fullness of this velvet moss shrinks and the colour dwindles and dullens to a yellow-stained olive. It is in late autumn and early winter that the moss changes, comes back to health, and gives out one of the most extraordinary green glows of any plant that exists – a sight recorded with fidelity and subtlety more than a hundred years ago in the watercolours of Samuel Palmer. If, as I suppose it must do in the next hundred years, this most ancient, primaeval business of roofing with thatch at last disappears altogether from England (it is about the one thing an inhabitant of the Saxon 'tun' would recognise on the Ash tree Tun, now, in the twentieth century), then Samuel Palmer's few watercolours of thatched roofing will remain as a record, as a sad record, of one of the really remarkable beauties of the English farm. As the *Tortula* thaws on a roof after frost, half the clump will be white still, and from the white shimmers that rounded, purest emerald. Thatch holds on, all the same. In this district it does happen to be more threatened than elsewhere. But if one drives in the early autumn through Somerset, Dorset and Devon, for example, it is surprising to number the thatched buildings, the newly thatched buildings, the thatchers actually at work, with a mass of clean straw at the bottom of the ladder. One gets the impression that thatch has died out more in sentimental accounts in books than it has yet in fact upon English buildings.

Along the cliff, thatch is still abundant enough to continue to be an element in the scenery, though it survives more on the chalk cottages, and more on farm buildings than on farmhouses. With expert thatchers so few, the roofs get a rough first aid. The gullies are patched up, or sheets of galvanised iron are thrust under the decaying eaves – either way a postponement of the end, of an end not so very far off. Before long, each farmhouse here will be surrounded by ruination; and after ruination – the visual unit of tradition will at last disappear. The old farmhouses will be surrounded by galvanised or asbestos roofing and concrete blocks, or they will vanish as separate farms (as perhaps they ought to), and be merged into larger and more efficient units. Either way, the visual loss, the visual break will be the same. Tomorrow's farmsteads will look as graceless as small factories; though the change may at least be some gain in the neighbourhood's social vitality.

The dangers of fire – hard to forget, if you live under thatch – and the recurrent expense of re-thatching were no doubt the motives – to which 'standing' and fashion might be added – for the wide introduction of stone tiles (which have a mediaeval as well as a Roman history in England). But under the cliff there can have been no authentic, early tradition of stone tiling. Eight miles away a little stone tiling was cut out of the hard limestone quarries; but it is some fifteen miles to the nearest of the regular old 'Tile quarrs'. Most of the tiles came from further away still – twenty to thirty miles; so, with conservatism, and the comfortable warmth of a thatch house to strengthen it, it is no wonder that so much thatching has survived, that tiles were seldom or never used here on cottages, and that on some of the farmhouses, as at Ashton, they were often used only on a part of the roof; only, in fact, upon an addition. The intricate building of these roofs was not a mere mason's work – professional 'tylers', or 'tylers with mortar', were at work around here at least on the church roofs by 1650. This addition at Ashton is later than that. It belongs to the eighteenth century; and it certainly looks as if the farmer had planned to have all the thatch removed, and the whole roof tiled. Three chimneys rise from a large hearth (into which was built a wrought-iron hearth-crane of intricate design with curling foliage) and from two coppers; but these chimneys were never raised clear of the thatch. They have been in use (until lately) for the best part of two centuries, and by good chance the thatch has escaped a fire. On several more farmhouses a back part with a loft has been added in this fashion (I shall explain why later on); and on their stone-tiled limestone roofs there is usually a large hummock of houseleek, which grows well with moss, lichens and yellow stonecrop – that plant known in one southern county as 'welcome-home-husband-though-never-so-drunk'. The tiles themselves are indestructible; but their weight has created another problem of decay. The timbers they are fixed to have sagged, and this has made openings under which the rain can drive. Proper repair would be expensive, would involve new timbering, and a search for a mason who still can manage this ancient craft of the tiler's. So the roofs continue to sag. The roofs are repointed with cement, and the wider gapings are

*Thatch on a stable. The final stage in pits and valleys
with a thick growth of plants.*

blocked up, and the owners continue to hope against the inevitable. One roof which had begun to sag was the stone-tile roof of the village church, erected only a hundred years ago. The stone tiles were removed (but for the few lower courses) and then replaced hideously with dark, square, brick tiles, whose regularity clashes with the variety and irregularity of the stone tiles below, clashes with their colours and the lighter colour of

The stone-tiled roof of the cheese-loft added to the farmhouse in the eighteenth century. The wall below is chalk, washed with cement.

the limestone casing of the church. This was a bad sample of botching, of the new loss of sensitivity to material and its tones. The truth is, the stone tiles are going, and I am not sure that the thatch, which they came to supplant, will not outlive them after all. To judge them from their present condition, by their present rich overgrowth, it must be the best part of a hundred years since any new stone tiling was carried out. Stones, slates and brick tiles (there are a good many brick tiles on local farm buildings, plain or pantile, and, like the bricks, locally made) may in themselves be everlasting and efficient in as much as they keep out the weather; but they certainly are not so efficient as thatch for keeping in and keeping out the warmth.

Whenever the word 'thatch' is mentioned, someone will still say 'cool in summer and warm in winter'; just as someone will say, when hedgehogs are mentioned, that gypsies cook them in clay. But about thatch, the truism is abundantly true. No other form of roofing, do what you will, makes life underneath it so pleasant. Fragments fall on to the plaster above the ceiling, and so may add to the amount of dust in a house, particularly in an old house (under the roof of Ashton Farm itself half an inch to an inch of debris from the thatch lies over the ceilings); thatch is indeed more liable to catch fire, thatch does indeed add to insurance policies, thatch does indeed decay, and need renewal; but the substitutes do not make you more comfortable inside. Pass in winter from the thatched portion of Ashton into the stone-tiled addition, and you feel the difference of temperature. In a stone-tiled house the bedrooms are chilly, in a thatched house warm, from the air of the heated dwelling rooms and kitchen below. One might think human skill could have devised or would still devise, a roof-covering with this great merit of the oldest, most primitive form of roofing in architecture, which acts as a species of porous woollen outer vest. It could. But oddly enough human skill seems to work, for example, by replacing woollen curtains with plastic curtains which tear, and refuse to check the draughts, and look cheap, and are cheap. One must remember cheapness and changes in the history of building. So, as things are, when thatch does at last vanish, a comfort and a healthy temperate atmosphere as well as a visual delight will have gone with it. Or maybe the whole world will enjoy central heating, and enjoy some device for deflecting heat in the hot months.

Upright from a fallen barn, carved with farmworkers' initials.

OAK, GALVANISED, CONCRETE

TIMBER, like most of everything else, comes now from outside. But it is reasonably certain that the timber 'carcass' of the farmhouse and its fellows was locally grown, felled and seasoned. Not, until lately, having the status of a parish, Netton next to Ashton has lost the craftsmen it possessed no doubt in its early manorial days. It had a mason, it once had a smith, it has a hedge-carpenter, but within memory it never had a sizeable carpenter's shop; never had a wheelwright; the only relicts, in this sense, of its manorial structure were the mill and the miller. (The manorial records of a neighbouring parish mention, among the mediaeval services, not only tending the ploughs, but providing the ironwork of the mill.) The bicycle age gave the village a bicycle shop, which has since developed into a garage, a hire service and a small fleet of buses; but that is all. Most of the carpentering, building and blacksmithing were centred in the two parent parishes; and two miles away one of these carpenters, with a small building business, does still survive. The carpenters of the two larger villages must have had plenty of good timber to draw upon. Elm is still plentiful, oak rather less so, though a good many straight-trunked, sturdy self-sown oak trees grow along the cliff, and down on the clay. The surviving carpenter buys his wood from the town, and the sawpit has long fallen in. The wood – he does not build any coffins – is all soft wood, since ninety per cent of his work is repair work, ten per cent the putting up of ready-made gates, ready-made sheds, outhouses and so on. And where, even thirty years ago, the carpenter would have been called in on the farm for repairs, very often now the farmer will improvise. One of the principals of the big barn at Ashton decayed; the farmer cut it out, and fitted in a secondhand railway sleeper. A good many old carpenter-made gates and gateposts still exist, of good oak, like the old squeeze-bellies; but they are replaced, when at last they decay (if indeed they are replaced), with these ready-made gates from agricultural firms – gates which, made of less timber, have about half the strength and life of the old gates, and none of their personality of design. The farmer cuts ash poles for fencing, larch for posts, though, if yew trees are handy, he may cut good posts out of yew branches. And often, where he would have joined up the posts with ash, he uses barbed wire. On Ashton Farm, and elsewhere, as well as gates, there are still old carpenter-made fences of inch-thick elm boards, set clear of the ground, and wide enough apart to allow the air to flow in between them and keep them dry and hard. In stables and barns, one sees roughly fashioned wooden brackets, of a curved branch in a single piece, nailed to the principals, or on to the solid weatherboarding: on these, horse collars and harness and ropes and odds and ends were hung. The weatherboarding itself was elm, and it decays slowly, remaining hard even as it wears away. When the holes in the weatherboarding get too big and cowshed or barn too draughty, the farmer, as usual, nails a galvanised sheet across. A new board – never. On Ashton, there is a small engine, and a circular saw, which does induce the farmer to square off occasional lengths of timber from the farm, all of which come in useful for a job of botching; but for the most part the circular saw chugs on for cutting up logs for the fireplace.

The big wooden barns were built for the corn before threshing. One of the eighteenth-century reporters complains about this local habit, and complains because the wheat or other corn was not put up in ricks when it was carried, though he admits that the barns were well fashioned for their purpose. The weatherboarding begins, as I have mentioned earlier, only some feet up from the ground, above the footing of chalk or sarsen; draught, but not damp, penetrates the weatherboarding, and so the barns were kept fresh and weather-proof. Even inside these dark caves, the sheaves had a chance to dry out properly.

Visually, the timber carcass of the farmhouse itself does not need much remark. Outside not much timber is visible, except (somewhat decayed) at the gable-ends. Good oak, and, I repeat, rather too much elm were employed. Economy at times allowed more sapwood than was really sensible, and the rafters have too often been repaired with fir. Yet even when the timber is outwardly decayed, even when the structure is unroofed and in ruins after long neglect, it is often surprising to discover the toughness of the beams at heart. Oak and elm alike are often difficult to get through without a circular saw.

Three more materials must be included, because they belong so intimately to the stagnant period of patching – the period of the last thirty years or so. These are galvanised iron, concrete and Portland cement.

There are many things uglier than galvanised iron. It may be – it certainly is – a shoddy roofing substance. By contrast, it may offend because it has no thickness and solidity; and because it cannot last; and one does come to associate it with patching. But associations have not to be allowed too much power over the eyes. New or in decay, galvanised iron with its straight close lines, or its rusty shades of orange and dark red and brown, often most beautifully combines form and colour in its farm company with thatch and stone tile and pantile. Perhaps one needs to have had a period of 'abstract' patterning in European art to realise that even something so commonplace, so despised, has its own formal beauty. Looking down from the cliff on to the farmyard, I have often been delighted by the way the lines of the galvanised roof of the Dutch barn, standing at right angles to the brown covering of the old barn, and at right angles again to the galvanised on a waggon-lodge (older galvanised, and rusted) mix into a design. Up on the downs, a fine old barn crashed in a gale after soldiers had pulled out a piece of timber or two. The galvanised iron pancaked across the sarsen footings, and rises like a large but low tent out of the grass. Waiting to photograph this amalgam of parallels and vivid rust, on a morning of open and shut clouds, we realised how excellent galvanised can look, like an orange and black zebra. Moreover, though this is applying almost the microscopic eye, the rust pits into the iron, once the zinc has gone, so that decaying sheets have a distinct superficial grain. Vision apart, I still cannot help disliking galvanised iron, wishing that its use had never been necessary, and that it had never been invented.

Its pretentious name means nothing. Galvanised iron is simply iron coated with zinc. The first patent was taken out in 1837, and in its corrugated form it seems that farmers began to make use of it between forty and fifty years later. Builders I have spoken to near the cliff say that they first began to supply it during the 1880s. *The Oxford English Dictionary* gives 1839 for the first appearance of the expression 'galvanised iron' in technical literature, and then jumps across the century to a very apt quotation from Rider Haggard's novel *Jess*, published in 1887: 'The stables and outhouses were roofed with galvanised iron.' Haggard, who knew much about farming matters, mentions it in the novel, disapprovingly, as something new-fangled; and certainly from the 1880s onwards galvanised iron began to spread its conquest of the English farm. *Laxton's Price Book for Architects and Builders* gives the cost of galvanised sheeting – corrugated – as three and nine a ten-foot sheet, in the thinnest gauge, four shillings in medium, and seven and six in the thickest and strongest. This was in 1901. A ten-foot sheet would cover, when lapped, a little less than twenty square feet of roof. So, using the medium gauge, a sizeable barn could be re-covered with 900 sheets at a cost, forty-five years ago, for material alone of something like £225. Thatchers have charged more and more for their work, thatching takes longer, and thatch wears out more quickly than it did. So galvanised saved money and time, to which farm and landlord could add the satisfied feeling that the barn would not catch fire, when, say, the tall-chimneyed engine came round for threshing. On a barn, galvanised iron lasts fairly well by our standards especially if it is painted or tarred. Even then 'lasting fairly well' means fifteen years, or twenty at the most. Actually it is the wind, owing to the height of the barn, which usually lifts it off. But galvanised is next to useless for replacing thatch over cow-stalls unless it is painted (as very often it is not) with an oxide paint. The urinary damp coupled with the heat rising from the cows' bodies rusts and corrodes the galvanised within about seven years.

The farmers here have patched with galvanised iron in a score of ways; an

Galvanised iron thrust in under decaying thatch.

old sheet will join the end piece of an iron bedstead in stopping up a gap in the garden wall. A broken manger will be patched with galvanised. An old sheet will replace a broken division between two calf pens. Sheets will be thrust in a row under the mouldering eaves of thatch (where they rust very quickly); and when the Ashton barn caught fire galvanised was hoisted up to mend the burnt section, which no one thought of re-thatching. Many of the granaries on their stone stilts have been re-roofed with galvanised, the sheeting and the weatherboarding tarred to match. And so on: galvanised iron came as a cheap godsend to farmers and landlords in a time of depressed, confused and subsidised agriculture.

Galvanised iron will be less and less used, as the later roofing materials of asbestos and cement, and one plastic kind and another, become universal;

so perhaps we are seeing now the last of the vividly coloured expanses of galvanised in decay; we are seeing the last of an inferior element of the picturesque, which will need explaining to our grandchildren. The sad thing is that the old buildings in the weakness of their age were patched with a material in itself so transient.

Like the invention of galvanised iron, the invention of Portland cement, and with it the invention of modern concrete, goes back a century at least. Its history, in modern times, can be pushed back still further to Smeaton's eighteenth-century efforts to discover a good 'water lime' for building the Eddystone lighthouse. Many other experiments were made, until in the 1840s (see, for a good account, John Watson's *Cements and Artificial Stone*) the true Portland cement was discovered by I. C. Johnson, when he was busy on the problem, through an accident of firing in one of his kilns. Johnson was manager of a cement works on the Thames estuary, and 'about the year 1845, his employers were in a position to guarantee a regular supply of reliable Portland cement'. All the same, it was nearly eighty years before the use of concrete (Portland cement mixed with an aggregate) penetrated as a building and patching material on to the farms. One builder here states that he did his first concreting on the farms – in any considerable degree – about 1920; and he gives as the reason that before 1918 Portland cement was often of poor quality, and unreliable. Hand-mixing was not well done, and the proportions – and the different proportions for various jobs – were not properly understood. John Watson in his book, which was written in 1918, remarks upon frequent failures in concreting, but puts it down with some reason to poor manipulation rather than poor cement; since here again was a technique which had to be learnt. When concrete did at last come in, everyone took to it, on farms, and in cottages, since with its aid much can be done for little money. There is no difficulty about getting a load of ballast – of gravel – delivered; no difficulty in getting the paper sacks of the cement, a hundredweight of which goes a fair way.

The use of concrete one can divide half-and-half between patching and improvement – a concreted cowshed means cleaner milk, a concreted farmyard less dirt and muddle. Board and joist floors badly laid and destroyed by dry rot, the replacement of broken-down steps, or a dry path in the garden – concrete is the universal answer; and for concreting, the farmer no longer needs the builder; he does the job himself, with his men, hiring, if need be, a mixer. He knows the proportions. He knows the tricks, but as I mentioned in the chapter dealing with chalk, he sometimes mixes up a concrete with blocks of chalk broken up fine. I have seen such concrete used in farm buildings. If one of those buildings caught fire, I fancy that concrete would turn rapidly into dust.

Concrete, one must say, cannot even claim the usual advantages and merits of galvanised iron. Its use maybe is a stage nearer to the factory farm, but if one wishes to sense the cleavage between the niceties of the old and the crudities of the new, then look again at the limestone panel in the chimney of the Ashton farmhouse with its double border, its 'R H 1934' rudely scrawled in the concrete steps which go up to the house.

Portland cement is also now the universal basis of all mortaring jobs. Everyone still remembers the use of lime and sand instead of Portland and sand; but they believe, wrongly, that for building repairs the new material is always absolutely the better. In his book *Our Building Inheritance* – a sensible, unsentimental plea for the preservation of buildings in the vernacular styles – Mr Walter Godfrey advises against the use of Portland cement and sand for repairing the mortar joints of old houses. They 'harden quickly and do not bind well with the old material. A mortar of lias lime and grit not only thoroughly seals the joint but it has no disturbing effect on the brick and stone surfacing.' But nothing that anyone says will change matters. Portland and sand are inevitable, as inevitable as aspirin for headaches. They go into every repair, in a method, right or wrong, which nothing now can shift.

How durable the new kind of concrete-block building which goes up on farms would be, in comparison with the old buildings of stone, or chalk, or brick, or sarsen, in comparison even with the oaken barns, one cannot say. Workmanship will have as much to do with it as materials, no doubt.

Granary of elm-boards above an elm fence. The boards have been tarred.
On the south-west side the boards are stained with algae.

TREES

REVERTING from the mere materials, the new and the old, to Ashton Farm, as it lies in its wide and intimate landscape beneath the cliff, how does one explain both that trees were planted here and that planting has long ago ceased? Fundamentally no doubt trees were a necessary crop, when timber was needed in the farmstead and round the farm for a thousand uses. An eighteenth-century tenant of Ashton would have thought it exceedingly odd that his twentieth-century successor would wield an axe by means of a handle of hickory imported from North America. He needed timber, and he grew it, and must still have done a good deal of planting, a good deal of conserving.

Writing in *Silva* about the walnut, John Evelyn says that 'in several places betwixt Hanaw and Frankfort in Germany, no young farmer whatsoever is permitted to marry a wife, till he bring proof that he hath planted, and is a father of such a stated number of walnut trees; and the law is inviolably observed to this day, for the extraordinary benefit which this tree affords the inhabitants.' That represents the old spirit – or three-quarters of the old spirit; since the other quarter must be that trees were *felt* to be desirable, as well as useful, that trees around a farm not only gave timber, and firing, and shelter, and shade, but united buildings and countryside, gave one satisfaction, marked the seasons by the fall and return of leaf. Trees were both right, in fact, and useful and a source of income.

Looking on to the farm and the village and across the plain from on top of the cliff, it does still seem that there are trees in plenty, that the darkness above all of the English elm in winter and its green in summer still muffles and modifies the rectangular scenery of the fields. Yet there must have been an extraordinary diminution of trees hereabouts since the eighteenth century. It so happens that a record has been published by the historian of one of the cliff parishes of the number of trees on thirty-five small holdings, from a survey made somewhere about 1710 or 1715. In all, the trees numbered 1,145, counting only oak, ash and elm. He estimates that now, on those same holdings, there are not more than 200 trees – in other words the three principal economic species have been reduced in just over two centuries by more than four-fifths; and the reduction goes on and on, every year. Ash trees are scarce, though this farm received its Saxon name of Ash tree Tun – Aesc-tun – presumably from their prevalence. But ash and the soil agree with each other, and plenty of ash poles grow in the hedgerows. Oaks are left alone, but there are not many of them. Elms have suffered by felling, by disease and by storms. An autumn storm in 1946, for example, uprooted hundreds of elms in the district – no fewer than twelve in a mile and a half of lane. Yet, as I say, elm still dominates the landscape. It is the English elm – *Ulmus procera* – peculiar to England; and its uses on the farm were innumerable. Evelyn talks of elm being employed in the seventeenth century for mill timbers, and especially the ladles of the mill wheel, for weatherboarding, for wheel hubs, for gates, for the kerbs surrounding a copper (where the wood would continually get damp); and, of course, it was, as it still remains, the timber for coffins. Great amounts must have been needed for the houses and farm buildings, for beams and flooring, especially in the barns.

The oaks are the remnant both of planting and of the original forest on the clay in which they were the dominant species; and John Aubrey maintains that this countryside produced 'as good oakes as any in England'. Nothing was 'so well qualified', as Evelyn says, 'to support great incumbencies and weights; nor is there any timber so lasting, which way so ever used'. Oak carries the main weights in the farmhouse, straddles, for example, the great open hearth under the essential chimney. Evelyn's list of the uses of oak includes the casing of cider-mills 'as best enduring the unquietness of a ponderous rolling-stone', shingles, pales, laths, cooper's ware, clapboard for wainscotting, wheel spokes, pins, pegs for tiling – a list which one could multiply without end. The laths under the thatch are oak, the older farm gates are oak. The substitution of so much elm for oak in the houses themselves must have been due to scarcity as well as expense, since Aubrey, in the seventeenth century, talks of the 'great plenty before the disafforestations'. Oak floorboards are scarce, though one farmhouse some miles away is oak almost throughout – floors, joists, stairs, banisters, panelling, doors. On the other hand, oak was used for the threshing floors in the barns, thick oak planks laid on oak sleepers which would soon rot under the floors if they were of any other wood.

Some elm is still used by the farmers; but very little oak. The third of the principal timbers, ash, the name-timber of the farm, is still the one most in demand, as it was in Evelyn's day: 'Carpenter, wheelwright and cartwright find it excellent for plows, axle-trees, wheel-rings, harrows, bulls . . . also for the cooper, turner and thatcher; nothing is like it for our garden palisade-hedges, hop-yards, poles and spars, handles and stocks for tools, spade-trees, etc. In sum, the husbandman cannot be without the Ash for his carts, ladders and other tackling.' Every 'prudent Lord of a Manor', thought Evelyn, 'should employ one acre of ground with Ash to every twenty acres of other land'. The farmers indeed still care for ash, in the shape of the long poles from the hedges, are still careful to preserve the stumps they grow upon, still employ them in abundance for fencing and railing.

After ash, oak and elm, the trees along the cliff next in importance were the willows, hazel, yew, and as it grows in the ground, whitethorn. By the streams which trickle out from under the cliff, there are still a good many willows – White Willow which pushes out white roots into the water, and Crack Willow which pushes out red roots – most of them pollarded so that they make their growth above the stretch of a cow's neck. Thatching 'spikes' or spears were, and are, made from these pollard willows; the wood was used for hurdles, and the trees performed the function of binding the stream banks and the edges of ponds. But most of the existing pollards are old and decaying, hollowed out in the centre, and soon likely to fall. No successors are planted. Here and there are some osiers, here and there even a neglected

Interior of a barn with its massive elm timbers.

osier bed. One basket-maker still continues to work out on the plain, making fine strong bushel-baskets which will give six or seven years' hard use. Grave mounds, formerly (as in the poem by Browning which I quote in the chapter on lichens), were carefully tucked in with osier rods – a practice which now seems to have disappeared in England.

Round here, next to no hazel is coppiced; but hazel again had its use in hurdles, in making wattle for wattle-and-daub (for which, as we shall see, willow was also employed), in thatching; and it was used, says Evelyn, for divining rods. The use of hazel for pea sticks is going out. More and more farmers and cottagers plant the dwarf varieties, and let the pods dangle against the wet soil. I have mentioned the planting of yews for windbreaks on the south-west of farmhouses and cottages. Evelyn remarks on the excellence of yew for 'posts to be set in moist ground', as well as for 'everlasting axle-trees'; and its durability is still well understood. Yew posts are still malleted into the ground and joined up with barbed wire. The chalk cliff is a natural habitat for yew; even if the farmers are afraid of it, afraid for their horses and cattle, the yews at least seed themselves, though none is planted. Whitethorn hedges are still general, still looked after, though barbed wire between stakes will eventually divide field from field, unless shelter is an absolute need. Larch, I repeat, has been planted at Ashton Farm, though the larches are now fairly old. Larch stakes and barbed wire are an inseparable pair. Yet most of the larch stakes on the farm are purchased, and not grown, not felled from the plantation.

The timber from many other trees must have gone into one thing and another upon the farm. There is usually a crab apple or two nearby (seedlings from the orchard), from which flails were made, as well as the silent cogging for mill machinery, for which apple wood is still normal. Maple grows well under the cliff into a tree, not merely into a bush, but it finds its way only into the fireplace. Sycamore is cut for runner beans, and bundles of sycamore rods spotted with a coral fungus lie about on the naked gardens in the winter. Guelder rose and quince trees are common, and in old days (according to Evelyn once more) one provided the pins for ox-yokes, and the other provided ox-goads. The farmworkers during the winter hedge-laying

Elm-board divisions outside calf-sheds, patched up with an ash pole.

will cut out walking sticks of blackthorn or briar. Holly is scarce; seldom, incidentally, producing berries. The flowers on one tree are usually all male or all female; and the trees here are too scattered for fertilisation. For the ubiquitous elder, the weed among trees, the companion of nettles, I have heard of only one early use (unless one counts the making of elderberry wine): in the cheese-making days in this district elder leaves were spread over thick, old cheeses in the cheese-lofts to kill or prevent the mites.

Evelyn, alarmed at the disappearance of English hard woods, put it down not only to the appetite of shipyards, iron works and glass works, but to what he called the 'disproportionate spread of tillage'. Many thousands of hedges, much hedge timber, must have been destroyed between 1939 and 1945, as hedges were skilfully grubbed up in a new spread of tillage. Now that the sentiment for trees has become rare – I know of few being planted along the cliff within the last thirty years except for a single avenue of horse chestnuts – now that the need for them alongside houses is no longer felt, now that so many are valued only as firewood, now that there is so little planting, and, owing to cattle and rabbits, so little regeneration by nature, now that so many of the existing trees are past their maturity, one must expect that the cliff and the plain will rapidly come to look barer and barer still, more and more drearily clean-shaven. When I hear a Christmas farmer talking ponderously on the air upon this earth, and this England, and its everlasting scene, I think of council houses without a shrub to modify their rawness, of elms standing up dead, or blown over by the wind, and pollard willows, tinderwood within, which seem to stand up only by their bark. When trees were appreciated as trees and valued for timber, when farmers held their farms on the old copyhold system of tenure for several lives (there is much to be said for the provisions in the new Agricultural Act governing tenure and relations between landlord and tenant), then it was worth maintaining trees, worth planting for one's grandchildren. In our time, whether one is tenant or farmer, the view is limited by the limits of the individual's own span. So who would plant trees, either for his pleasure or his profit, when he cannot live to see them?

The disappearance of trees fits in well with galvanised and concrete and botching, with the uncertain spirit of an age between ages.

WATER

No LANDSCAPE is a landscape without trees; and no landscape, the artist Samuel Palmer held, whatever its attractions, is perfect unless it gives the glint of water; and one might add to that the sound of water. By those tests the cliff landscape scores, if a pass at all, only a narrow pass. I have pointed out that the settlements along the cliff were made where the springs emerged between chalk and greensand. Most of the streams are small, fall fairly quickly for a hundred yards or so across the talus, singing in a quiet tone which is audible at any rate on a still night in the rainy months, and reaching the plain, become the sluggish inhabitants of long, deep ditches, marked with willows and sallow, and now and then a marsh-marigold swamp.

The flora of the streams is not very rich. Willowherb is typical, valerian, meadowsweet – but one misses such plants as watercress and mimulus. On the plain, the streams silt up their ditches which run along often under tunnels of ancient whitethorn and blackthorn, marking the boundary between farm and farm. Prisoners of war have been turned to cutting and cleaning these watercourses, and from the mud thrown up on to the banks one can often pick out pieces of mediaeval pottery. In summer, the springs get low, the watercourses will dry up, and the landscape, but for a willow-edged pond or two, can seem waterless indeed. Down over the cliff there are dry, water-carved gullies, damp below the surface, which occasionally change into noisy torrents when storm water collects up on the wheatlands, and pours over the lip. But whatever the appearances are, however low the springs get, until the steady arc into the trough becomes only a slow trickle of green slime, the supply never gives out, the wells never get dry, and the green meadows never get brown and yellow with drought. The grass immediately below the cliff has a lustre and lusciousness which is absent further out on the plain, and the cream-line on the milk shows the difference.

The water is not utilised as it might be, and as it indeed must be sooner or later on the farms. Wherever they can, the farmers bring the water indoors, and also carry it to an improvised dairy-shed, where it runs down over a milk cooler. On one farm the water drops three or four feet between the orchard and the stackyard. A concrete path turns down into a dell across which slopes an elm tree. Under the elm the milk cooler is fixed, the farmer wheeling the churns to and fro on a trolley. These cliffside farms, all the more so now that so many of them have lost their upper wheatlands, must continue (so long they continue at all as separate farms of the same genus) to depend in the main upon dairying. Though cheese-making here goes back at least a hundred years earlier, it was in the eighteenth and through much of the nineteenth century that almost all the milk went into cheese, which explains the cheese-lofts, and the big coppers, and the stone-floored dairy-rooms which opened straight on to the farmyard, for the convenience of bringing in the milk. It was a good cheese, described in 1789 as being 'in the first estimation among those who indulge their appetites' with 'a richness, and at the same time, a mildness, which recommends it to many in preference to that of Gloucestershire'. Or rather, it was several kinds of good cheese. Cheese was made throughout the year: soft, thin cheese in the spring which went up every week to London, loaf cheeses and broad cheeses. Winter cheese was scurfy and white-coated, and so coloured red before it went to the factors. That, at any rate, belonged to the eighteenth-century practice, as it was described by the agricultural reporter upon the district in 1789. There are men of seventy now alive who remember their mothers occupied with nothing but cheese year in, year out; but towards the end of the nineteenth century, though not all at once, the cheese-making had died away, as the London demand for milk began to increase. The milk, not collected as it is now by factory

Cattle trough, fed by the foundation spring of the farmstead.

lorries, was driven into the station by the individual farmer. The change from cheese to milk improved matters, so Richard Jefferies maintained in *Hodge and his Masters*, afforded more labour, brought waste land into grass, caused new seeding on the old fields, and draining. Cowyards were repaired, and the breed of cows was improved. 'Nowhere', said Jefferies, 'was the farmer more backward, more rude and primitive, than on the small dairy farms. He was barely to be distinguished from the labourers, amongst whom he worked shoulder to shoulder; he spoke with their broad accent, and his ideas and theirs were nearly identical.' Jefferies may have exaggerated the degree of improvement; but he was speaking generally of a wide district, not particularly of this small and peculiar district. Here the changeover from cheese to milk took place, altering the inhabitants and raising the status of the farmer, but not, it seems, to such a degree. The farmer has been a milk farmer now for some seventy or eighty years, and so water supplies are one of his great problems by present-day needs; and here he is not in a very much better case than he was in 1890 or 1900. The ancient spring of the farm may supply his house, his dairy shed and his milk cooler, and give him, piped, enough supply to wash off the cows and swill out the cowsheds; but though the water is available, on most farms it is not piped into field troughs (though the fall would make matters easy); and in summer the ponds and the natural trickles dry up.

Still, the farmer outside the village is better off than the farmer in the village, and better off than the villagers. He can equip himself with a bathroom and usually a water closet and build himself a septic tank below the house in his own field, without interfering with anyone else, crossing into anyone else's land, or infringing any by-law. In the villages – in particular in the village alongside Ashton Farm – good water is indeed piped out of the large spring and into the farmhouses and the cottages; but these Netton houses are built left and right from the road which follows the line and descent of the stream, along the small gully. One householder could only build a septic tank in another householder's garden below him. There is no public drainage, so earth closets or chemical closets are still the rule; and the water from the household sinks is carried off in old square stone-floored and stone-roofed drains to join the central stream; into which a farmyard or two drains as well. Or where there are no sinks, the water is slopped out of doors on to the garden.

Either way, beside the road an evil-smelling fluid moves off down to the plain. The by-law will not allow this to be augmented by wastage from baths fitted with plugs and water hot and cold. So the villages and the village farmers wash as their ancestors washed, from buckets or in tin tubs; and tubful and bucketful are tipped out into the drains. The people argue that there is no sanitary difference between the water from a tin tub and the water from an enamelled bath; forgetting that their zeal for cleanliness is slightly checked by the trouble of filling and emptying the tin tubs. Allow bathrooms, by-law and sanitary inspector both argue, and the evil-smelling trickle would become an evil-smelling river.

Perhaps the situation will go on until an epidemic, though only the Second World War held up a scheme for drainage – a scheme which is now shelved *sine die*. But Netton will be a pleasanter village when a pure brook tinkles away beside the road, with the stones visible through its waters, now grey and soupy, when one can walk to the public house or the post office unassailed by smell.

If a water diviner were to shift to and fro over the talus slopes below the cliff, round the farms or round the village, his hazel rod would be wagging and twisting. A farmhouse or two may be on a dry sandy platform; but most of the houses are built upon dampish ground; and this spring-fed, underlying moisture is responsible, as well as age or poor materials, for the poor state of many of the cottages, several of which were condemned, and saved from demolition only by the war.

Lichens on brick.

LICHENOLOGY

If one forgets every association, every other element in the appeal of farmstead, cottages and village, and looks simply at what is, excludes concrete and repairs and looks for modifications of surface and looks for colour, one realises how much the attraction of this country architecture depends upon time and growth and the softening of lines, whether growth of surrounding trees or growth of lichens,* which I have so often mentioned, or moss. How much, in fact, depends upon an equilibrium between life and death, liveliness and decay.

Lichens, for example, spell decay, eating their way how slowly into the limestones which a great many species prefer.

Where every condition is suitable for their growth, where there is damp and light, crusty lichens will cover even transient objects quickly enough. On the shingle, for example, of a beach in the Isles of Scilly, above the mark of the highest tides, I have seen an old boot turned into gold by lichen; but under the less favourable conditions of the mainland, it takes a good time for lichens to modify the natural tones of a brick or a stone wall or a new roof of slates. In fact, the *Handbook of British Lichens* records of one species that it increases in diameter only by a centimetre in a year; so even if lichens spell decay, their destructive rate upon buildings is something one need scarcely worry about.

---

* Botanists, dictionaries and pedants talk unnaturally of *liken*. Those who are alive to their own language forget the Greek original and talk naturally of *lichen*. Who now says *kinema*?

Lichens can stand extremes of damp and dry – provided the damp and the dry are mixed. What they cannot stand is dirty air and an absence of light. They cannot stand the smoke of large towns. Search for them as you will, not a patch of thin gold or grey will meet your inquisition in London, or in Sheffield, or in Glasgow; lichens are pre-eminently something of the countryside, something natural to the Ashton farmstead, rejoicing in such buildings as an extension of their natural home on rock or tree – just as swallows and martins have found artificial caves and cliffs in cowsheds and under the eaves of houses.

Yet lichens are part of that great host of living things mankind refuse to see and distinguish and familiarise by common names, confining themselves to the obvious, to flowers, birds, mammals, insects and reptiles – to those things, in fact, which they can use as symbols. It is true that scientists, artists, poets and connoisseurs of the picturesque developed a fancy for lichens in the eighteenth century. James Sowerby drew and painted many species with an exquisite precision for his great volumes on British botany, on either side of 1800, when the classification of lichens was still crude and partial.

The Rev William Gilpin recommended lichens as an element of picturesque beauty, in which he was followed by Uvedale Price. There were ruins enough in the countryside in their eighteenth-century day, but the vernacular traditions were still alive; for them, luxuriate in its picturesque qualities as they might, a decaying barn or cottage could not yet have that melancholy of a dead, or dying, culture which now stares one in the eye up and down England. The connoisseurs, and with them the artists and the poets, belonged to a time when the irregular was supplanting the regular, when emotion was supplanting reason, when biology was getting more adherents than mathematics and astronomy.

In 1797 the artist J. T. Smith published a small book with twenty etchings of cottages, which was called *Remarks on Rural Scenery*. After dividing cottage scenery into two classes, 'namely the neat and the neglected', we artists, says Smith, 'turn from this neatness and regularity, to what *we* must esteem a far more profitable subject – the neglected, fast-ruinating cottage – the patched plaster, of various tints and discolorations . . . the weather-beaten thatch, bunchy and varied with moss – the mutilated chimney top – the fissures and crevices of the inclining wall – the roof of various angles and inclinations – the tiles of different hues – the fence of bungling workmanship – the wild unrestrained vine.' All these adjuncts, and more, 'offer far greater allurements to the painter's eye than mere neat, regular, or formal arrangements could possibly have done'.

That is the state of mind in which lichens, which are so much a part of this farm scenery, were examined, admired and brought into poems and pictures. Poets who celebrated lichens include Coleridge, Southey, Crabbe, John Clare (who even knew their bitter taste, or more probably the taste of the green alga, *Pleurococcus*) and Robert Browning:

> See, as the prettiest graves will do in time,
> Our poet's wants the freshness of its prime;
> Spite of the sexton's browsing horse, the sods
> Have struggled through its binding osier rods;
> Headstone and half-sunk footstone lean awry,
> Wanting the brickwork promised by-and-by;
> How the minute grey lichens, plate o'er plate,
> Have softened down the crisp-cut name and date!

That is Browning, in a poem he published in 1845. Fifteen years before, Samuel Palmer had been seeing lichens on the bold trunks of the oaks in Lullingston Park, on wooden fences and on thatch. Ruskin, tidying and gathering up after his predecessors, delighted in the colour of lichens, and wrote, but wrote well, of them as though his had been the first eyes to detect them upon tombstones or upon alpine rocks:

> When all other service is vain, from plant and tree, the soft mosses
> and grey lichen take up their watch by the headstone. The woods, the
> blossoms, the gift-bearing grasses, have done their parts for a time, but
> these do service for ever. Trees for the builder's yard, flowers for the
> bride's chamber, corn for the granary, moss for the grave . . .
> Sharing the stillness of the unimpassioned rock, they share also its
> endurance; and while the winds of departing spring scatter the white

Stone tiles covered in lichen and moss, while the roof timbers beneath are decaying and breaking.

hawthorn blossoms like drifted snow, and summer dims on the parched
meadow the drooping of its cowslip-gold – far above, among the
mountains the silver lichen-spots rest, star-like, on the stone.

Pre-Raphaelite painters accepted lichens as a paintable detail of
nature, with all those other details of the natural scene which they
picked with such moral fidelity and transferred with such unimaginative
fingers on to their canvases. The Pre-Raphaelite time, in fact, produced
the only attempt there has been at a popular handbook of lichens, by
the distinguished lichenologist, Lauder Lindsay. He quotes from Crabbe
about 'Nature's ever-during stains', about the stone where

Science loves to trace her tribes minute,
The juiceless foliage and the tasteless fruit;
There she perceives them round the surface creep
And while they meet their due distinctions keep,
Mix' d but not blended: each its name retains,
And these are Nature's ever-during stains.

It was in the Pre-Raphaelite time that a party of Cornish lichenologists
met – it was at Penzance, I think – to partake of an experimental lichen
supper, of leathery fragments, either bitter or tasteless.

But from the 1850s onwards – though the study of lichens has gone
on, though their nature as a partnership between fungus and alga has
been discovered (the lichen algae, the green 'weather-stains' on wall and
paling and weatherboarding, are also a portion of the colour of farm
architecture), though the lichen flora of the world has been explored
– from the 1850s, lichens have dropped out of common experience,
dropped out of sight. Lauder Lindsay wrote a sad paragraph, introducing
his *Popular History of British Lichens*, which though true in general,
was not so true of the sixty or seventy years preceding his book.

'They have ever', he said, 'been the acknowledged *opprobria* of
Cryptogamic Botany. The delicate waving frond of the fern is anxiously
tended by jewelled fingers in the drawing rooms of the wealthy and noble;
the rhodospermous seaweed finds a place beside the choicest productions
of art in the quilt and broidered album; the tiny moss has been the theme

of many a gifted poet; and even the despised mushroom has called forth classic works in its praise. But the Lichens, which stain every rock and clothe every tree, which form *nature's livery o'er the globe where'er her wonders range,* have been almost universally neglected, nay despised.'

Yet if one takes an interest in vernacular building, in the buildings along the cliff or anywhere in England, one must take an interest in the lichens to which so much of the beauty of their texture is due, to the differences of the lichens on tar-sprayed weatherboarding of granaries and on brick, on chalk and the harder sarsen, which allows a foothold for fewer species; on sarsen and the lime-mortar, spotted with yellow which outlines each block. All we lack for that interest (and someone should provide it) is a popular accurate account of the common species, explaining the strange nature of the lichen-plant in its symbiosis of a fungus and an alga, with coloured plates as pleasant as those pioneer drawings of lichens by Sowerby, even if such plates can only be a rough and ready index to the difference between species and species.

We owe much to lichens. Photograph after photograph of those which we took to illustrate this book show lichen on brick, tile, on wood and show now and then the green 'weather-stains' of algae – growth, all of it, which unites the buildings to the earth out of which they emerge; and it is true that lichens and algae and mosses will not despise concrete blocks and council houses. In time, they will do much to modify and decorate the worst banalities and machine-made *naïvetés* which are ousting the vernacular. Glossy wall surfaces and large areas of glass and plastic are not so likely to enter into farm building, so perhaps we are not so much in danger as one might think of living in a world minus the yellow and orange and greys and reds and greens of a lichen flora, minus colours that fade and brighten according to the weather-colours which symbolise an intimacy between ourselves and our environment. Lichens will survive, so long as we use stone, whether stone from the quarry or 'artificial' stone such as concrete. In the shape of lichens, the country may even invade the cities – will certainly invade the cities – when at last that abatement of smoke which is possible, desirable and so much discussed, is in fact carried through. When J. T. Smith analysed his cottage-scenery, made his distinction between 'neat' and 'neglected', regular and irregular, he never knew the soulless regularity of a modern cowshed, a modern farmhouse or modern council house. Neat or neglected, his cottages, like all other buildings in the vernacular, were put together of basic materials which the builders themselves modified and regularised only to a degree. That the buildings along the cliff seem to grow out of the ground as well as be imposed upon it, is partly because of the growths which time has now put upon them, and partly because the builder shaped his own materials, or had them shaped for him, without a rigid dictatorship of feet and inches. No two bricks from the old kiln up on the downs measure precisely the same, or match precisely in colour. No two sarsens have exactly the same tint. The blocks of chalk (except towards the end of the chalk-building era) differ in the same ways. No two beams of oak were identical, no two stone tiles, no two weatherboards, no two chimneys, or chimneypots, or windowpanes, or window openings. Add all these up, and no two buildings in any category exactly repeat each other. So one pleases one's eye between the type and the specimen, continually. Moreover trees, and the configuration of the land around farm and farm, house and house, produce different effects, different lights, different shadows. The alignment of walls and roof in relation to north, south, east and west produces its different effects of weathering, its differences in the growth and colouring of the lichens, the algae and mosses.

Some of these differentiating, modifying agents of growth, of course, affect, or will in time affect, the careful and dull exactitude of the new buildings in the countryside. The lichens and mosses will break the exact triangular or rectangular wall spaces, correct (if that is not to use the word paradoxically) the exact repetitions of machine-made tiles. But split a human face down the nose from forehead to chin, and the two halves are never found to be identical. The human face and the older building are alike in that satisfying irregularity. The older building has just that amount of regularity which human contemplation can stand (and also needs), and just that irregularity which human contemplation cannot do without. A regularised, a mechanically measured, exact layout of farm and farm buildings may be a convenience to the farm; but it must be an offence where a natural irregularity exists all around. A single regular building in a medley of old buildings of the vernacular may have a measure of congruity by means of contrast, as when galvanised iron, with its narrow lines of light and dark, stands alongside thatch and tile, a pleasure to the eye I have already spoken of; but heaven help us when every farmstead has become indistinguishable from every small factory at Slough: it will not be the pleasantest interim period in English life. Heaven help us, if ever the ruler of the Roman road or the steel tape-measure of the intersecting straight lines of the American city becomes the dictator of the countryside – if we are forced, in part of our lives, to be divorced any further from our natural environment.

Ruination. The end of a thatched cottage built of brick and chalk.

THE RUINS

ᚷᚱᚨᛏ ᚠ ᚱᛖᛞ

R UINS ANYWAY – and all the more if we are indeed beginning to live out
of our natural environment – are valuable to us. They provide us with
something we need which is more than a gentle melancholy, a mild chance
of morbidity. We need their symbolism of transience, however skilfully we
attempt to hide, however skilfully now we cover up the full stops of life.

The symbolism of ruins in English literature begins, I suppose, with that
Anglo-Saxon poem which is held to describe the abandoned Roman city
of Bath: 'The grasp of the earth, stout grip of the ground, holds its mighty
builders, who have perished and gone; till now a hundred generations of
men have died. Often this wall, grey with lichen and stained with red,
unmoved under storms, has survived kingdom after kingdom; its lofty gate
has fallen . . .' Poets of the eighteenth and nineteenth centuries thought
particularly upon ruin and flower, and a ruinous building does work
its healthy function in human feelings and thought, not only because
it shows death, but because its death does nourish these lichens and
these green algae, does nourish this moss on the thatch, this rosebay
willowherb on the beams, does give birds places where they can build
in the cracking walls, does give crannies to insects, from the bee to the
woodlouse. For us, in our disorder, our muddle of disintegration, a ruin
should give special delight because, beyond symbolising disorder and
death, beyond nourishing wildness, it yet imposes some order on that
wildness, some order of the rectangularity of walls, the triangularity
of eaves, the parallels of the roof-timbers half concealed, half shown.
This way of regarding a ruin adds something to the clergyman-poet,

Langhorne, for example, writing of wallflowers upon a ruined tower rising in Milton's 'vegetable gold', in obedience to Nature's command that they should bestow their 'honours on the lonely dead'; adds something to that slightly saccharine poem (which I have always been fond of) by the sad Hartley Coleridge, in which he compares his unsuccessful being to an 'aged rifted tower', covered with flowers:

> Hast thou not seen an aged rifted tower
> Meet habitation for the Ghost of Time,
> Where fearful ravage makes decay sublime,
> And destituted wears the face of power?
> Yet is the fabric deck'd with many-dappled hue,
> Gold streak'd with iron-brown, and nodding blue,
> Making each ruinous chink a fairy bower.
> E'en such a thing methinks I fain would be,
> Should Heaven appoint me to a lengthened age:
> So old in look, that Young and Old may see
> The record of my closing pilgrimage:
> Yet, to the last, a rugged wrinkled thing
> To which young sweetness may delight to cling.

In another sonnet Hartley Coleridge speaks of himself as a 'patch of dusky snow in May'.

An anthology of ruin or old building literature of Romanticism, to which the Langhorne and the Coleridge both belong, would include much from the systematisers of the picturesque, from Gilpin, that is to say, and Uvedale Price; much from other, greater poets (especially Crabbe, with his gleaming eye upon weather-stains and lichens and church towers), much from such artists as Cotman among the churches of East Anglia, Cotman feeling himself into the surface, the grain, the colours of the stone of arches, the timber of beams, the plaster of walls. When such men wrote of ruins and painted ruins, they were more freely open to the winds of experience than I think we allow ourselves to be. They were divided between past and future, between an enormous, an intimidating future, and the ordered past of calculation and common sense which that future was pounding into scraps. They were divided between the solidity of land and the incalculable movement of sea. We are divided; but we are far less agreed about past or future, far less able to see, with a consensus of vision, either what the future is likely to be (or what we should prefer it to be) or what the past, the immediate past, actually has been. Death, and such a symbol of death (and therefore of life) as a ruin, we have been inclined to turn away from, in order to contemplate a factory block or a double row of builder's Tudor, bordered with truncated limes. In England, until the war, ruins were scarce in towns and cities. It was a relief to go from London into such a city as Worcester where some degree of natural shabbiness, the natural squalidity, of old buildings replaced London's new bakelite smoothness, which denied that either man or building could die. Have you ever seen a dead man in London? A sixteen-year-old child, or man, in the London of 1560, or 1660, or 1760, or even 1860, would probably have seen the London dead a good many times. Now, if a man should die of heart failure in an A B C, one can hardly blink before an ambulance (dial 999 for police, fire brigade or ambulance) has whisked up from nowhere and whisked the dead man off to an invisible mortuary slab. When Herman Melville came to Liverpool as a young seaman, the bodies of the drowned were exposed in a Dead-house, in the basement of one of the churches, until they were claimed by their kin, or taken off for burial by the parish. 'Whenever I passed up Chapel Street, I used to see a crowd gazing, through the grim iron grating of the door, upon the faces of the drowned within. And once, when the door was opened, I saw a sailor stretched out, stark and stiff, with the sleeve of his frock rolled up, and showing his name and date of birth tattooed upon his arm. It was a sight full of suggestions; he seemed his own headstone.'

We conceal death, conceal it from ourselves. In the town near the farmhouse, in the cemetery where the dead are buried in numbered graves, laid out in rows as if the graves were the houses they had lived in thrust down into the ground, they cover the raw, inconvenient earth with a carpet of artificial grass – while the funeral goes on. We conceal death; and we try to conceal, or at least arrest and tidy up our ruins. Old ruins we hand over to the National Trust or the Office of Works; in the way that we rid ourselves of learning by handing it over to the universities, or the arts by handing them over to a gallery, or religion by handing it to the parson. Symbolic ivy is removed, the walls are pointed, the ruinous essence is extracted and thrown away. This ruinous essence concentrates obviously in this one fact, that the building – castle or abbey, or whatever it may be – is in movement, is moving slowly through Hartley Coleridge's 'closing pilgrimage from life to death'. Each century (that is the point) should create its own ruins; for by arresting the pilgrimage we falsify antiquity and cheat ourselves. We imagine to ourselves that we immobilise and embalm the present, and stabilise the past.

In fact, for ruins proper, for the inexorabilities of decay, for the pleasures and satisfactions, that additional satisfaction of order in disorder which they can legitimately give, we must turn now, in England, from the grandeur of abbey and from the grandeur of castle ruins to ruins of cottages and farmhouses. (Blitz ruins are another thing: the essence of a ruin, again, is that time, and not explosion, or incendiary bomb, length of time, slow, and not a minute or two seconds or a second, should have been the agent of ruination. Yet Blitz ruins have no doubt done some good out of their evil.) With humble ruins, humble, genuine ruins, we have to be content. They are the best just now that we, or time, can do.

Actually, as several things I have said will now have revealed, final ruination comes rather too quickly here under and along the cliff, owing to the preponderant use of chalk; which, hard when protected, vanishes or turns into a mound when it is not, only a little less quickly than the cob of buildings in Devon and Cornwall. The wooden beams often last longer than the chalk walls, and lie about among the nettles which grow out of the chalky disintegration. Cottages have often been built into the slope below the cliff. Long before they are deserted the gardens have slowly shifted and piled themselves up on the chimney end, and the ground level has risen under the windows, making the cottages still more damp than they were, still more liable to ruination.

The ruin I have most watched, been most absorbed by, is the ruin of 'Bubbe's Tun', farmhouse and buildings alike; but there the quick pace of ruination was finally quickened by man. When I knew the farmhouse to

Elm timber from a fallen barn.

begin with, some twelve years ago, it had been re-roofed with galvanised iron; and a farmworker and his family lived there. The galvanised, anyway, was its warrant of execution. Then galvanised iron became scarce, and the farmworker having left, the sheets were ripped away. First to feel the weather and feel it severely was, as it happened, the brick portion added (like the brick portion at Ashton Farm) in the nineteenth century. The bricks were good, the construction was not so good; and whole sections of walling quickly slabbed to the ground. The nineteenth-century elm timbers had neither the bulk nor the durability of the timbers at the chalk end of the house. The panel doors did not last on their hinges like the older batten doors at the other end sturdily hung with band and hook. But pretty soon rain and frost began to devastate and tumble the chalk on to the overgrown flowerbeds. The outside walls split and fell, the outer ends of the huge, still hard oak joists crashed with them, bringing the bedroom floors down on a slope. Pushed off, a climbing rose sprawled among the mess. Inside, the division walls were made in two ways in this older portion of the house. Some – presumably the older ones – were wattle-and-daub, once known in these parts as 'freething'; some were brick-nogging – bricks, that is to say, laid herringbone-wise within timber frames. The daubed wattle-work in this house was not made, by the way, of hazel, the only wood mentioned for this purpose in book after book upon building construction, but of some species or other, so Kew determined for me, of willow – willow with the bark left on, still hard and sound under the plaster after 300 years or more. Duck's-nest fireplaces of the early nineteenth century hung rustily and coldly in the bedroom walls, one filled with the sticks of a jackdaw's nest. Layers of wallpaper peeled off in the rain; but the bottom-most layer was never of a very old pattern. A few iron bedsteads had been left behind, and some old boots, and a tin chamber pot. Last to fall – it is still there – will be the enormous, weighty, solid chimney stack. True, it is made of chalk, but its base is protected by the debris of the floors and the walls, and the brick cap and a side shaft of brick give some protection up above. The chalk, never exposed until now, has a naked unnatural pallor. Grass seed has been taken by the wind to the upper steps of the chimney, but the grass dies and dries away quickly in the summer, though it keeps vivid below on the remains of the bedroom floor and the staircase, where its roots are moistened and away from the sun. Beams have broken off and their stumps jut out from the chalk. In the middle of the house, in the middle of its façade which looks over the plain, the oak panelling of one small room still clings to its wall; and on some of the beams rosebay willowherb has found decay enough to root in, and to mature. Perhaps within three or four years – perhaps sooner – the chimney stack will have crashed, and the whole ancient house will have become a mound – a nettle mound, with roses, laurel, balm, soapwort and periwinkle on its fringes; and still, outliving the house, the two or three yew trees will continue at its south-west corner, between house, as it once was, and the ageing, decaying, blue-tit-frequented apple trees.

I have spoken of the pathos of two tags of telephone wire hanging from the chimney. Also, pathetically, on one of the last bits of chalk walling on the north-east of the house, is a fire-insurance sign, a rayed sun dated 1827, fixed there against a calamity which never happened, a premature death; a precaution curious to contemplate upon a ruinating scrap of a house.

Nearly all the farm buildings have crashed into a mess of decaying wood crossed by the rusty straight lines of their sheets of galvanised; but it still, I think, will be years before the overturned granary of tarred elm-boards disintegrates and deprives the white owls of their nesting home.

I met not long ago a man in his early middle-age – a farm-advisory officer who had been born and brought up in this house, many times gone up and down in the waggons from the now overgrown stackyard to the 'white lands' above, by the track which curves down through the cliff. He was the last of a large family of children who were all born in this place which had been so humanised for more than 700 years. The balm I crush and smell in my garden comes from Bubbe's Tun and I have grown a rose bush, with white, silvery, globular, briar-smelling flowers, from a cutting off the thorny sprawl by the front door. Somewhere, I fancy, beneath all the debris, sealed in now for ever under the nettles which are already liberal, is the well of the house into which the water will still be trickling out of the base of the cliff just behind.

And it occurs to me that the church – where, on the floor, stretches the mediaeval brass of a former owner of Bubbe's Tun, 'preserved' under coconut matting and trodden on by the boy who blows the organ – that this church is every bit as much of a ruin, spiritually, for all its careful and tasteful restoration, as this pile of chalk and timber and brick and willowherb and old bedsteads.

The process of falling to bits reveals many facts of construction. One can see, for example, at Bubbe's Tun what shallow notches were cut in the big beams to hold the floor joists, letting the joists into the hard oak only an inch or so. As one low wall of the barn alongside has opened up (long ago it had lost its thatch and been covered with galvanised iron), one can discover how carefully the raised 'mow' or threshing floor was laid. First of all brick piers were built up from the ground, some eighteen inches high. Across these stretched the joists which carried the thick, two-inch boards. Where the boards joined, strips of wood were nailed along underneath. The cracks between the board and board would soon pack up over these strips with chaff and fragments of straw, and no grain could drop through. (According to Thomas Davis's report for the Board of Agriculture, drawn up in 1794, most of these threshing floors were laid on to sleepers – which is so at Ashton Farm – ie on to beams which rested direct on the ground, or at least on flints and broken cinders through which the rats and mice would not penetrate. But here there was no ground level enough to build a sizeable barn, so the brick piers could not be avoided.) One must remember that these threshing floors had to stand up, resiliently and firmly, to the thumping of the flails. The boards had to be thick, the cracks had to be properly sealed, and sealed underneath in a way that the flails could not damage. Threshing with the flail I have never seen; but I remember those lines by Stephen Duck (a poet who was born and worked as a farm labourer not so very far away from the cliff):

From the strong planks our crab-tree staves rebound,
And echoing barns return the rattling sound.

We are so used to the hum of the threshing machine, the dust hanging in the sun, the open-air bustle in the stackyard (all that, too, will give way to the combine harvester), that we forget how ancient is the why and wherefore of these great barns which have now so long outlived their proper use. To think of threshing machine, barn, flail, is to realise with a new freshness how much farm buildings, as they still exist, belong to our earlier, pre-mechanical farming, to realise why it is that neither farmers nor landlords are too inclined to spend money on the upkeep of antiques which are more useful for storing the lumber and the odds and ends of farming than for much else. The stable-end of the Ashton barn still serves, of course, in lieu of a better stable; but the great roomy barn itself, while sheltering a tractor and implements of one sort and another, and also housing some calf-pens, is mainly filled up with sacks of cement, sheets of galvanised, coils of barbed wire, odd lots bought at sales and never used, and miscellaneous rubbish which is as well there as anywhere else. Had the fire from the engine of the milking machine actually destroyed the barn, the farmer would have been more than reconciled by now, and free of the worry of keeping – or not keeping – the great roof in repair. As the wet gullies pierce the thatch, will it be pulled off and replaced by sheeting? Even that would be a messy and long job. So the skeleton of timbers will just decay and sag and crash.

Meanwhile, to get these barns with their tough threshing floors really sharp in the focus of time, perhaps it is worth quoting a bit more from Duck's *Thresher's Labour*. The labourers go off to their barns – here to the wheat barns, there to the barns where the barley is stored. The farmer says:

'So dry the corn was carried from the field,
So easily 'twill thresh, so well 'twill yield,
Sure large day's-works I well may hope for now.
Come strip and try; let's see what you can do!'
Divested of our cloaths, with flail in hand,
At proper distance, front to front we stand.
And first the threshal's gently swung, to prove
Whether with just exactness it will move:
That once secure, we swiftly whirl them round,

From the strong planks our crab-tree staves rebound,
And echoing barns return the rattling sound.
Now in the air our knotty weapons fly,
And now with equal force descend from high . . .
In briny streams our sweat descends apace,
Drops from our locks, or trickles down our face.
No intermission in our work we know;
The noisy threshal must for ever go;
Their master absent, others safely play,
The sleeping threshal does itself betray . . .
Week after week we this dull task pursue,
Unless when winnowing days produce a new:
A new, indeed, but frequently a worse!
The threshal yields but to the master's curse.
He counts the bushels, counts how much a-day,
Then swears we've idled half our time away;
'Why look ye, rogues, d'ye think that this will do?
Your neighbours thresh as much again as you.'

Duck describes the work as one who had suffered from it. Cowper, in *The Task*, describes it as a spectator:

                    Wide flies the chaff,
The rustling straw sends up a frequent mist
Of atoms, sparkling in the noon-day beam.

But adds:

Come hither ye that press your beds of down,
And sleep not; see him sweating o'er his bread
Before he eats it.—'Tis the primal curse,
But softened into mercy; made the pledge
Of cheerful days, and nights without a groan.

Duck would have agreed less on the cheerful days, but fully on the primal curse. His description makes one less inclined to look back regretfully to the period when the farms now in decay were built; and built well, and worked as a social unit of validity. That long, that weeks-long, primal

The last of a barn: built with sarsen footings and elm-boards,
re-roofed with galvanised. Finally blown over in a gale.

curse is one which the modern farmworker is well without; on some of the
bigger farms hereabouts the threshing with the flail went on for most of
the winter; remembering that, and remembering Stephen Duck, one can
understand why the fairy thresher in the barn occurred so in folklore.

Not far beyond this threshing floor, not far beyond Bubbe's Tun, a
thatched cottage of the kind that the Stephen Ducks of the cliff were born
into and in which they died is now coming apart. Nothing much is left
in the garden except a shrub of a rather dull species of *Lonicera*, and
clumps of a cultivated dead nettle with silvery, variegated leaves, a bay
tree and a plum against the wall. The thatch has nearly gone, revealing the
roof timbers and the transverse strips of oak, and also the galvanised iron
which as usual was thrust in under the thatch below a window in the eaves.
The thatching spears stick out of the brown like quills all about. Around
and below one window, below a hole in the thatch, last winter's frost has

brought down the outer chalk skin of the wall, showing (in contrast to the construction of the farmhouses) how flimsily these cottages were built. Only the chimney and the brick quoins are keeping the building upright. The porch in front is made of galvanised iron painted red, the path to the gate (edged with the pink-flowered, silver-leaved dead nettle) is made of the customary sarsen (though many of the cottages under the cliff are approached simply by a mud path, as though the farmers never thought of sparing part of a load of sarsen for their workmen and their wives). At one end of the cottage, in a lean-to, a finely built chalk oven – a bread oven – projects from the wall. It is built of pieces of chalk squared to about brick size. The shape is that of half a cylinder with a top curving inwards. The cottage was inhabited till 1940 or so; but I doubt if bread had been baked in that oven for fifty years.

Earlier on I described the stable-end of a barn nearby, which has now crashed and been cleared away. I had hoped to save from that a memento which went back into the eighteenth century, a piece of boarding upon which carter after carter had carved names, dates, initials, and had incised a drawing or two – some of horses, another of a gallows with a rope. But out into the rain the boarding went with all the other timbers. The farmer, perhaps, had never even looked at it. I went into the stable of concrete blocks and asbestos roof which supplanted the end of the old barn. In the old barn the stables had been floored neatly with sarsen. But nothing at all of the old was used in the new. The sarsen had been concreted over. And the new concrete stable, with its rigid roofing and steel windows, efficient as it may be, simply has the character of mensuration – smooth walls and straight lines. It is not akin to human, or to the merely animal, or to the living stall. It might have been put up anywhere from Missouri to Siberia. In fact, like many council houses, it differed only from a hovel because it was a building of straight lines, an efficient building dependent upon the improved industrial techniques which have produced the materials. The old building was human, was the work, from thatch to sarsen, from central oak pillar to the gallows on the boarding, of individual men. The new building, techniques apart, is naive, uncultured and raw. It will never be within its power to decline into a ruin of dignity and spirit. The date '1946' has been rudely scraped with a stick into the wet concrete of the doorway just as a date was scrawled into the concrete steps at Ashton; and in that alone one can understand the double influence upon each other of a tradition and the material employed in that tradition. The traditional materials are hard, but manageable; but the managing took time, trouble and understanding. Cut a date in stone, and the stone has something to say about the letters and the figures. All that the wet, flabby concrete says is, write, and do the little best you can. When a barn was built of chalk and timber, chalk and timber were managed on the spot by the craftsmen and their inclinations, peculiarities and personal pride, managed according to their nature and the nature of their materials, within the tradition. The builders of this new stable received their concrete blocks ready made, of a standard, identical size. They could do no more with them than build as a child builds with wooden bricks. As a child I recall being irritated with bricks because of their intractability; because I could not divide a brick in half; because their sizes were fixed. Hence the childishness, the naivete, the ugliness, the coarseness, of such modern farm building. When time gets hold of them at last, they can only be a little less dull in decay than they were in life, they can only, lichens and so on apart, be like a brick building in a nursery which has been half kicked over. Styles of building, Lisle March Phillips says in the *March of Man*, 'act over again, in a sort of Dumb Crambo, the history of their time'. What a different history is acted by the dead vernacular of the cliff and the new factory universality which is replacing it! In the days of the vernacular, the cottages were known by the people who lived in them. Nowadays all the cottages have been numbered: a letter is addressed to 'Mrs Shefford, 87 Netton'. The council houses are built in blocks of two together. They are built without regard to the villages as existing units of character, which have slowly developed, without regard to the other houses, the positions of post office, inn, church. To be in love with a building. Can one be in love with a council house? In love, as a farmer or a farmer's child, with a congeries of concrete slab shippens and stables, with asbestos roofs around a concreted farmyard?

Bubbe's Tun. Bedroom wall of wattle and daub at the head of the stairs.

INSIDE THE HOUSE

IT IS TIME to go indoors, into a house which shows that no remark has ever been farther from the truth than that 'a house is a machine for living in'. It would be as true to say that pants were a machine for walking in, or a bed a machine for sleeping in. But it would be true, true indeed, to say that a house is a second suit of clothes, that a good house conforms to human bodies individually and socially, and also conforms, so to speak, to the emotional and rational projections of the human animal. A hedgehog disappears into its grass nest, and gathers the grass round to its shape, in warmth and in comfort. Men and women and children enter into a house and gather it around them. But they must move within a house; not lying compact like the young of a hedgehog, they need space. So a doorway conforms to human physique: its height has come to be fixed just conveniently above the average of human height. Its width is just so much more than the average of human width. The door handle comes down the door to a point convenient for the hand as it hangs down from the shoulder. Everything thus conforms, or should conform – the height of steps, the height of windows in relation to one's eyes both standing and sitting, and so on. A wide open hearth presupposes several pairs of feet stretched towards the fire. Close it in, insert a Victorian or a modern grate, and you presuppose a smaller, divided community, with servants in the kitchen and children in a nursery; and social distinctions. The shape of a room relates itself subtly to the human shape and human needs; the walls must be so arranged, containing doors, windows, fireplace, in their relationship, not only so that one is left free to move, but so that the mind is left its freedom, is given its proportions, its satisfactions; while mind and body are yet walled in with comfort and protection. The perfect room, the perfect house, strikes an average between the convenient and the agreeable, with an infinite number of adjustments and modulations, which the building crafts have learned unconsciously, or at the most, half unconsciously, to provide by generations of activity and experience. Houses, particularly houses in the vernacular, have been built appropriately without knowing how, just as George Sturt's wheelwrights built a wheel without being able to explain how they built it, without being able to analyse it step by step. The human body, the human *being*, the family, the social pattern – far from being machines or mechanical, it is around all these that the houses of a people have grown, a house such as the one at Ashton. If the walls come too close, human need and human feeling push them off again. If the walls go too far, or the ceiling goes too high, human need and human feeling call them in, or down.

A very clear proof that in the nineteenth century the norms of human development were interrupted is often a nineteenth-century room – a room which has lost all emotional contact with those who are to live within it. Many nineteenth-century houses and houses since the nineteenth century presuppose some animal of a different species, whose highest value is the pretension of a class in relation to the class next below. The obvious necessities are not forgotten: the house has a roof, walls, doors, windows. The doors are tall enough and wide enough; the stairs, step by step, are high enough. But the subtleties are succeeded by barbarity. Rooms are wrong, wrongly shaped, wrongly proportioned; often because it was wished to make the rooms, indeed the house, pretend to a certain level. So in such a building, sitting in such a room, one often feels uncomfortable, and ill at ease, as a grown-up gibbon must feel when it is first confined in a cage. The proportions of a room can interfere at this point and that can deprive the mind of its balance and its rest. The room becomes to the spirit like an ill-fitting shoe to the foot. It raises spiritual blisters, whereas the necessity of a good shoe is that the foot should be unconscious of any surrounding leather. I have known a small living room in a cottage of the plainest, crudest kind, which, taking its shape, its proportions, from centuries of tradition, can absorb five or six people in comfort and with satisfaction; whereas a room many times larger will seem awkward, irritating, cramping, simply because it abuses this well-balanced relationship between the inhabitant and its own bounding surfaces. One recalls once more that remark of Lisle March Phillips's that the 'styles of buildings act over again, in a sort of Dumb Crambo, the history of their time'.

The farmhouse, one discovers quickly, possesses this relationship to those who live within it. For the most part, it is emotionally and physically right; and it was right in its day for the particular functions of a farmhouse, as apart from the general function of a house in its kinship of wall and ceiling and space and so on to body and mind. Yet I ought to say that all is not exactly right with the nineteenth-century addition in brick.

That needs entry and explanation. The front door, where the eighteenth-century porch had been, opens into a hall, flagged with squares of sarsen. Beyond, a door opens into the kitchen, and beyond that again a second door opens into the back-kitchen, equipped with the two coppers. From this back-kitchen one walks, right, into the farmyard or, left, into the vegetable garden.

Back in the hall, between the front door and the kitchen door, but on the right, one enters a stone-flagged dairy. On the left in the far corner, up go the stairs. Alongside, between the stairs and the front door, a fourth door in this hall enters into the two rooms added somewhere about 1870 or 1880. These additional rooms, fitted with wires leading out to bells in the kitchen, mark a nineteenth-century division, more or less the completion of a long process, between farmer (and farmer's wife) and the farm servants. The rooms were added after that changeover from cheese dairying to milk dairying. Certainly a room had existed here before in place of the two rooms. The first of them is small, with only one window which faces north-east – it is the room in which the farmer does his books, fills in his forms and writes his letters, and it has an unnatural shape; it has a disagreeable narrowness across the width of the house. Till lately a small cast-iron fireplace was let into that side of the room which divides it from the hall. The wallpaper was perpetually damp on the left and right of the fire, until the fireplace was removed, revealing behind its iron face and behind brick walling that chalk-flanked open hearth, with its great oaken bressumer. When the nineteenth-century workmen filled this hearth in, their work was done so poorly that quantities of old and new soot descended into traps which they left upon either side, and the soot was made damp by the rain which dropped down the great wide chimney. Ten barrow-loads of wet soot were wheeled away.

From this first room a door beyond opens into the sitting room of the farm. This again had only a window facing north-east, until the farmer some years ago had a second window cut, facing south-west, and letting in the afternoon sun. The sitting room is not disagreeably proportioned; but it suffers from being an appendix of the house, from being so far distant from the hall and the kitchen.

Originally, there must have been one fairly large room on this side of the hall, not quite as large perhaps as the two rooms combined, but a room focused around the chalk-walled oak-beamed hearth. The relationship of room to hall and kitchen was then unimpaired. One other point. Kitchen and back-kitchen as well as hall and dairy are flagged with sarsens. These two additional, later rooms have plank-and-joist floors. The floors were badly laid, ill-ventilated, the joists in one of them actually resting on the soil, actually parallel to the wall ventilators, so that the air could not circulate from side to side. The technique again was not understood; and both floors have suffered from dry rot. Moreover these nineteenth-century brick walls rise direct from the soil without damp courses and without sarsen foundations or footings. So the walls are damper than the old chalk-upon-sarsen walls of the rest of the house. Rose-tree roots wriggle in under the bricks and grope whitely beneath the floorboards. In fact, these two rooms, damp, ill-adjusted to the house, with their windows ill-arranged, exemplify that break in tradition, that nineteenth-century interruption in the pedigree of living; these cold stone floors which sweated may have become a mark of poverty, to be superseded, as they themselves had superseded the hard-earthed floors which survived so often in the farmhouses till the sixteenth or the seventeenth century.

Compare with these rooms the wide, if somewhat low, kitchen. To begin with it runs north-east to south-west. The morning sun comes in through the window in the southerly wall. The sun moves away, towards the heat of noon, and then, in the late afternoon and evening, it comes in cheerfully once more through the window in the westerly wall – a humanly perfect arrangement, for comfort of the body and the spirit. Ignoring this, a farmer in the 1920s cut off the southerly window by a matchboard partition, making a passage between hall and back-kitchen, and turning the kitchen into a dark little den, cheered only by the evening sunlight.

It is not entirely easy to unravel the old scheme of the house before the gentility of nineteenth-century farming upset the past. But at one time the house seems to have consisted of the present hall, the dairy on the right of the hall, a large living room with the open hearth on the left of the hall, and the present kitchen, with perhaps a small 'back-house'. At one time, it is clear, a door opened out directly from the dairy into the cowyard. This nucleus of the house as it now is would be the house as it was after being refashioned by 'RS' in 1668; the house as RS refashioned it round the still older core of the sixteenth century, of which the base of the chimney and the big fireplace were remnants.

Then, as the cheese-making became more important, and the London cheese trade increased, in the middle or just after the middle of the eighteenth century, the present back-kitchen, with its well and the cheese-coppers and, overhead, the cheese-loft, were added. Then, or later, they blocked the doors from kitchen and dairy into the cowyard. The back-kitchen in fact was provided as a cheese-room. The well one must suppose to have been there before, in the open, more or less; and since a well cannot be moved, and since one cannot do without water, the well had to stay. A sarsen trough was placed above it (with a stone drain leading under the floor and out into the large, square, stone drain flanking the cowyard), and above the trough a pump.

About now the house, at the other end, also received its eighteenth-century porch. The house of 1668 was thatched. The eighteenth-century cheese-loft was tiled, and since the chimney from this cheese-room was not carried above the neighbouring level of the thatch, it must have been the intention, as I have already remarked, to do away with the thatch altogether, and tile the whole building. Perhaps the necessary alterations for cheese-making cost too much. When the old room beyond the open hearth was pulled down a hundred years or so later, and the pair of new genteel rooms were added, with bedrooms overhead, the thatch was kept and extended at that end, gentility, too, having its financial limits.

Thus, as it exists today, Ashton farmhouse has grown and changed in answer to changes in farming and the social status and behaviour of the farmers. Yet on the whole the house has preserved its humanity, its function as an extra suit of clothes traditionally made to fit, at a distance from the body.

Upstairs, too, one can trace the alterations at the two or the three dates. A single flight of steps opens on to a small landing (the existing stairs are of plain nineteenth-century workmanship). The landing, a small bedroom and a large bedroom cover the two nineteenth-century sitting rooms. A doorway without a door opens the other way into what was the bedroom – the main bedroom – of the master and the mistress of the house. In this room, leading into the same great chimney as the open hearth downstairs, is the well-carved fireplace, in chalk, of the seventeenth century – in fact of 1668. From this room, as the house was then, three doors gave into three bedrooms, two of them small over the dairy, one of them large over the kitchen. These rooms are divided one from another by partitions of wattle-and-daub within timber frames. At some time before the nineteenth century, judging by the character and the sturdiness of the woodwork, the principal bedroom was divided by the present partition into a smaller room and an additional landing by which two of the bedrooms could be reached. But before that the lay-out was the normal one, with the master and mistress sleeping as guardians of chastity between the rooms occupied by the men at one end of the house and the women at the other.

At the far end of the bedroom over the kitchen a cupboard is cut out of the thickness of the older outer wall, the second chimney wall. This cupboard was lit by a window which now looks only into the gloom of the cheese-loft.

Fittings of various types and ages survive within the house. Contrasting with the tall casement windows and their large lights in the two nineteenth-century rooms downstairs and also in the hall, the windows in the kitchen are only two foot six high and have small lights; only a small sash in the centre opens, vertically; not by weights, since one slides the sash up and fixes it with an iron peg. Roughly made oak shutters close on to the windows from the inside, the folding panels fastened with butterfly-shaped side-hinges, nailed, and not screwed, to the wood. These are hinges of the kind which Joseph Moxon illustrated in the eleventh part of his *Mechanick Exercises* in 1679. Four sets of wall cupboards in the older bedrooms have oak doors of similar workmanship, with some hinges of the same kind. The window in the bedroom cupboard which now looks into the cheese-loft has a wrought-iron casement frame, nailed up, with small, square lights set in lead. All these odds and ends presumably date from the reshaping of the house in 1668.

In the eighteenth-century cheese-room and cheese-loft there is little detail to be marked except the unglazed windows of the loft, of oak with diagonal bars. The windows are closed with a sliding panel, and must have been survivors into this century of an older type.

Many of the nineteenth-century alterations have now been removed. All the iron-surrounded nineteenth-century grates have gone, except two in the bedrooms; but the ornamental graining in green and yellow and white paint upon the seventeenth-century chalk mantelpiece and upon the nineteenth-century mantelpiece in the bedroom over the kitchen has been left, and deservedly. That graining in imitation of stone (so much disliked by Ruskin) is still common in the neighbourhood. The small town nearby has an artist in the graining of doorways and shopfronts, whose work gives liveliness and colour to the one long street. White doorknobs and door-plates belong to the 1870s; together with the last two of the wire-pulled bells. All of the bells had a different pitch; the one with the deepest note was rung from the front door. One gentility – one gentleman's alteration, and a dangerous one – rose from the farmer's family of the '70s not liking the rough honesty of the walls. The hall was not treated too badly: it was plastered and pargeted into large rectangles. But staircase, landing, the small bedrooms – the irregularity of their timber-divided, plastered walls was too much; and they were covered in with thin matchboarding, behind which the elm was liable to rot. Most of this skin of gentility has now been removed again, and none too soon for the well-being of the house. Some of the bedroom walls and the kitchen walls had been papered, but their irregularities did not lead to a very neat job. None of their papers – the underlayers – was earlier than about 1880 (which was true of the wallpapers of Bubbe's Tun), as if the notion of wallpapering in those humbler farmhouses came in very late. Beneath the paper over the daub and the timber frame in the bedrooms the daub was stained a wintry blue. This was the orchil or archil dye, made from lichen, and introduced from Italy during the Renaissance. S. O. Addy in his *Evolution of the English House* (1898) writes of this archil blue still being used inside houses in the north of England. Other old walls inside the farmhouse were whitewashed under the paper and the matchboarding, the wash having been stained green in the bottom layer on the kitchen walls.

Until a few years back the generations of farmers and farmers' wives and servants had relied upon the well; but the water now from the spring which fills the cowyard pond – the original spring of the settlement – gets pumped up the cliff as far as the elms and piped down again to the house and the buildings. Yet even now there is no lavatory. Beyond the back-kitchen, or cheese-room, is built a lean-to; three quarters of it used for coal and wood; a quarter of it, walled off and reached by an external passageway roofed with slate and walled by a trellis of ivy, serves as a closet. It was a three-hole closet not so long ago, about a great pit emptied not as often as the nose required. A faint disturbing smell seeped under the yews and hung about over the grass in the stillness of hot evenings. The three-holer of old polished elm-boards at last has yielded to a chemical bucket and seat; and the primaeval smell has been exorcised. Externally what strikes one about the house, under its muff of rather coarse thatch, which curves round the windows and makes a curving line from gable to gable, is its straightforward seemliness, as though, once more, it had grown out of the ground. A rounded guelder-rose bush, a rounded clump of box in front, harmonises with the shape. The wind-breaking yews reach up above the thatch, and draw the house into their embrace. At the back, the small lawn between the sides of the L rises by stone steps, under a black archway of two yews, into the long kitchen garden, with its south wall of brick. Running parallel with the wall on the other side of the garden (which is divided up by a cross of concrete paths) stretches the cliff.

Internally, the house seems strong rather than elegant. The lines are seldom straight, the floors, except for the wooden floors in the nineteenth-century part of the L, slope downwards towards the cowyard. The impression is one of an inexpensive honesty. This and that has been scamped; yet even the elm and the sapwood which have decayed and have been replaced, lasted, it is well to remember, more than 250 years.

It is no longer easy, all the same, to see the house quite in its old authentic plainness. It is lit now by electricity, the walls are pink, or cream, or yellow, in place of the cold archil blue, the whitewash, or the green. In the kitchen there is now a sink, an electric water-heater, and an Aga cooker. Upstairs, one room has been changed from a crude shape of wattle-and-daub into a bathroom, with a water-heater, a basin and an enamel bath. All these additions, not to say the kind of furniture now in the house, from the Frigidaire and the wireless set to the curtains in the windows, are alien to its old nature. They conceal that the house was – in fact is – an unsophisticated product of the vernacular, a house which was occupied and modified by a succession of poorish copy-holders, in a poorish district. Moreover, the house, as RS finished it in 1668, may very well not have been painted outside, oil paint still having been something novel in his century. At the most, the woodwork would have been thinly stained with colour.[*]

---

[*] Innocent, in *The Development of English Building Construction*, states that bulls' blood was often used, and that oil paint, presumably bound with walnut-oil, was apparently first used on exteriors in the seventeenth century.

To contemplate this traditional simplicity and then to compare with it the urbane delicacies and graces of an eighteenth-century mansion, with its treatment of space and light and its cantilevered staircase, and its refined workmanship is to understand what architecture means as an art, to understand the difference between art and folk art. Yet to know architecture one needs to know both, to know the elegant, which often loses something of humanity, and the vernacular, which is the simple expression of the human need.

Many such houses as this one have become divorced from their farms, and have gone over to other occupiers. If they treat their ex-farmhouses with a sentiment near to the ridiculous at times, one cannot doubt that the houses give them reason for satisfaction and delight. In their plainness they have grown out of a plain, even a graceless culture; a culture, at any rate, not merely a civilisation; and they have, I repeat, grown round human beings, with everything that such a circumambient growth has caused. One cannot blame men and women for wishing to live in houses which do not sneer at their human status and their human necessities.

TRADITION

ONE WOULD understand Ashton Farm, the chalk cottages and all the buildings in this district under the cliff, understand all the details of their material and their construction, everything from the orchil-blue walls to the three-seater lavatories, everything about the tradition of the vernacular – understand them inside and out, only if one could understand, inside and out, the people who have lived here since the sixteenth century. To understand them as they are now would need years of study, and the result might indeed be 'too sarcasticall and offensive' to make it easy to go on living or showing one's face in the particular neighbourhood again.

Down here below the cliff or above, the conditions of soil and crops and labour and livelihood no longer affect the nature of the people so much, since their lives have become more independent of habitat and local produce. George Sturt wrote *Change in the Village* at the beginning of the twentieth century, of a less isolated part of England; and honestly and gloomily, and accurately, he pictured village life in decay. He wrote of generations of villagers who 'had grown up and lived and died with large tracts of their English vitality neglected, unexplored'. He wrote as someone disillusioned, who had once believed the English country to be 'the scene of a joyful and comely art of living', whereas he had come to know 'that those who live there have in fact lost touch with its venerable meanings, while all their existence has turned sordid, anxious and worried' – and, he continues, 'knowing this, I feel a forlornness in country places, as if all their best significance were gone'. He believed

that there had been a 'sturdy peasant civilisation', built up 'by the force
of its own accumulated traditions' – a civilisation now vanished; and it
was this civilisation which set up the farmhouses of Ashton and Netton.
Such views are usually blanketed and pushed out of sight by the pastoral
sentimentalists, who write on and on from a pale notion, and not from
the life, not from all that would stare at them if they opened their eyes.

Yet puffing and puffing does not puff the farms off the landscape.
Oddly, there is still thatch under the cliff as there was a thousand years
ago, when the Saxons, in their communal way, were farming the Ash
tree Tun and the Neat Tun; and for the time perhaps it is less aggravating
to think about what is and what was, than to speculate upon what the
English could do with fuming if only dung and reason and knowledge
could be applied to the fields all as easily as each other.

Contemplating the farm enables one to contemplate something of
the way in which men need the gyroscope of a tradition if they are to
live, or make, or build valuably. The bottom layers of traditional value
are necessary, too, for the top growths of genius. Even an Ashton
farmhouse has to do with the creations of the genius in architecture.
And if one stands back, and looks at the whole assembly of the farm and
its buildings, at their arrangement one against another, their placing in
the landscape, their setting in combination with apple trees, walnuts,
yews, limes, elm, if one considers them in time as well as spatially, in
their kinship to generation after generation of farmers and farmworkers,
and manorial lords and landlords, one must again realise how little
this agreeableness has come by conscious effort. All has grown, rather
than been determined by acts of will: the methods of building, the
organisation of the farm as a unit of buildings, can be analysed, but
never would have been analysed or described accurately by any farmer or
builder at any time in the long period of their formation. At no point was
such analysis or description necessary, when everything could happen in
obedience to needs, materials and an evolving sense of what was right.
If the farmhouse is durable, it is because such and such materials had to
be used, and because there existed a tradition of how to use them. Yet

The dying barn. Thatch and timber give way to concrete blocks and brick.

one must be careful of gilding one's ancestors with too much sanctity. In the farmhouse, after all, so much was done to save materials, so much for economy; and if the materials were of a certain standard, even if the builders and the farmers desired that standard, one may as well remember that the materials could not drop much below it. Ignorance about the exact strength of building materials acted on the side of virtue.

One must think, too, that when a tradition is strong and universal within its variations the craftsman is little tempted; he has seldom to choose between the good and the extremes of nastiness. Tradition helps the artist and controls the feeble; and when in the nineteenth century England abandoned 'sane and civilised building' through what Mr Walter Godfrey calls a 'dementia', tradition and its feeble charges together had been assaulted by new methods, new materials, new designs made available through education and publication-above all by new philosophies. If the strong resisted, the mass of men, the feeble, were naturally overwhelmed. Tradition had chosen for them, not taught them to choose for themselves. Tradition had managed the work, so to speak, or nine-tenths of it, and the tenth, in which the feeble had been inspired by tradition to manage it themselves over a small range, could not help them very much. It was like the Railway Mania. Suddenly, in and after the 1830s, it was possible to gamble in shares. The habits of morality had never been so stupendously tested in this way. So the temptations of money could not be resisted, so even the staid and the respectable fell in the new delirium; even the Duke of Wellington had to ask favours of Hudson the 'Railway King' when his sister was in trouble over her shares. An islander from Tristan da Cunha is liable to succumb quickly in Europe to diseases against which his body has acquired, and needed, no natural fortification. So it was with money, so it was with building.

We should not wish to preserve so much of what Mr Godfrey has called 'our building inheritance' if we were adding well to the inheritance by our own building and had been doing so for a hundred years. So one gets as testy, now and then, with the preservers as with the destroyers. The preservers get in the way of the living; their influence tends to perpetuate old modes and the imitation of the old. One suspects their 'taste', since a taste comes from a living and not from a dead tradition. The preservers are too often parasitic, in fact, upon dead tradition, and if, as some people think, world traditions of culture, instead of local idioms, are now being formed, these influential views, with their repetitive eulogies of the past, get in the way. It is difficult enough for traditions to drop their seed leaves and grow, more than ever difficult when changes are going on, social, scientific, industrial, changes in assumption, changes in belief, to confuse those whose adherence would help to confirm a tradition. The older building traditions grew like oaks or yew trees, slowly; forming hard, durable timber – in contrast to the conifers which grow quickly and uselessly, like fashion. The fallacy of the moment is that taste can be independent of a tradition, that human beings in schools can be taught to choose aesthetically between good and bad, as if an old tradition could be resurrected or a new one forced under glass within a few years. We could be happy if for every Ashton farmhouse which disappears, something better, and of our time, could go up; and go up as little noticed and as little conscious of itself.

THROUGH THE WOODS *H. E. Bates*

MEN AND THE FIELDS *Adrian Bell*

HAVERGEY *John Burnside*

ORISON FOR A CURLEW *Horatio Clare*

SOMETHING OF HIS ART: WALKING WITH J. S. BACH *Horatio Clare*

ARBOREAL: WOODLAND WORDS *Adrian Cooper*

ISLAND YEARS, ISLAND FARM *Frank Fraser Darling*

LANDFILL *Tim Dee*

HERBACEOUS *Paul Evans*

THE SCREAMING SKIES *Charles Foster*

THE TREE *John Fowles*

AN ENGLISH FARMHOUSE *Geoffrey Grigson*

TIME AND PLACE *Alexandra Harris*

THE MAKING OF THE ENGLISH LANDSCAPE *W. G. Hoskins*

FOUR HEDGES *Clare Leighton*

DREAM ISLAND *R. M. Lockley*

EMPERORS, ADMIRALS AND CHIMNEY SWEEPERS *Peter Marren*

THE UNOFFICIAL COUNTRYSIDE *Richard Mabey*

RING OF BRIGHT WATER *Gavin Maxwell*

DIARY OF A YOUNG NATURALIST *Dara McAnulty*

WHERE? *Simon Moreton*

SEA STORY *Louisa Adjoa Parker*

LOVE, MADNESS, FISHING *Dexter Petley*

THE LONG FIELD *Pamela Petro*

SHALIMAR *Davina Quinlivan*

THE ASH TREE *Oliver Rackham*

ANCIENT WOODS OF THE HELFORD RIVER *Oliver Rackham*

LIMESTONE COUNTRY *Fiona Sampson*

MY HOUSE OF SKY: THE LIFE OF J. A. BAKER *Hetty Saunders*

SNOW *Marcus Sedgwick*

WATER AND SKY, RIDGE AND FURROW *Neil Sentance*

BLACK APPLES OF GOWER *Iain Sinclair*

CORNERSTONES: SUBTERRANEAN WRITING *Mark Smalley*

IN PURSUIT OF SPRING *Edward Thomas*

ON SILBURY HILL *Adam Thorpe*

THE NATURAL HISTORY OF SELBORNE *Gilbert White*

NO MATTER HOW MANY SKIES HAVE FALLEN *Ken Worpole*

GHOST TOWN: A LIVERPOOL SHADOWPLAY *Jeff Young*

Little Toller Books
w. littletoller.co.uk   e. books@littletoller.co.uk